*A TAXONOMY OF COMMUNICATION MEDIA*

# A Taxonomy
# of Communication
# Media

Rudy Bretz
The Rand Corporation

Educational Technology Publications
Englewood Cliffs, New Jersey

A Rand Corporation Research Study

# Preface

This study was undertaken as a contribution to two Rand Corporation projects involving instruction and the communication of information. The first, supported by Project Rand, concerns Air Force instructional systems and ways in which they might be improved. The second, undertaken for the Department of Health, Education, and Welfare, is intended to assist the Lister Hill Center for Biomedical Communications of the National Library of Medicine in planning programs in support of nationwide needs for biomedical information. Specifically, The Rand Corporation is considering ways of improving the design of systems for technical training, of improving medical education and medical-information delivery, and of extending continuing medical education. All of these objectives involve applications of communication media in instruction and information retrieval.

Although much has been written about techniques of artistic expression in various media and about the social implications of the more pervasive of these, there is little of communication theory that is useful to those who must make decisions concerning the applications of the new technologies. It is to fill the need in this area that the present monograph was conceived.

I am indebted to my colleagues at Rand, particularly Polly Carpenter, for their patience in listening to my arguments, reading my material, providing constructive criticism, and contributing insights in subsequent extensive discussions. This has resulted in not only a sharpening of the thinking involved, but also the addition of important elements to the argument. Also helpful were Matthew Reilly, Leland Attaway, Ann Summerfield, Harold Steingold, George Comstock, Arnold Chalfant and Sam Bar-Zakay.

The draft manuscript was carefully read and reviewed by Robert Specht and J.C. Shaw of Rand, for whose comments and contributions I am also grateful; I am similarly indebted to Michael Bretz of the University of Washington, Harold Wigren of the National Education Association, Ken Winslow of the Ampex Corporation and Edward Stasheff of the University of Michigan. The contribution of Janet Murphy, a Rand editor, rates an honorable mention. I would like particularly to thank C. Ray Carpenter of Pennsylvania State University and William Paisley of Stanford University, who were kind enough to review and comment extensively on the completed manuscript.

This monograph is but the first phase of a much more extensive treatment of the subject. It is limited to defining the media themselves, and describing the characteristics of each medium that determine its best uses. Subsequent phases will consider the effectiveness, flexibility, accessibility and responsiveness of the media, and their adaptability to the individual needs of the learner. Feasibility considerations will also be examined, such as costs and benefits, standardization, equipment reliability, staff training requirements, demand and acceptability.

Rudy Bretz
The Rand Corporation
Santa Monica, California

September, 1970

# Abstract

This monograph defines and describes communication media; discusses the difference between information and instruction, instructional media and instructional aids; and proposes a set of criteria by means of which communication media may be distinguished from nonmedia, one medium distinguished from another, and a single medium distinguished from multimedia applications.

A two-dimensional classification system for communication media is proposed: in one dimension, seven classes are defined, based on ways of representing information; in the other, communication media are divided into two groups, telemedia (see Glossary) and recording media.

The author has directed this work more toward media users and professional practitioners than toward scholars or researchers in the field. As much as possible, standard audiovisual terms and phrases have been used. Since there is wide variation in the meaning of even the most common communication terms (e.g., message and media), each term is defined when it is first used, and to emphasize its importance, a glossary is placed at the beginning of the monograph.

Twenty-eight specific communication media are defined and described. This list includes the major available and soon-to-be-available media. Since the entire communication field is in a state of rapid growth, both in the development of systems and in their applications, it is to be expected that revision of this list would be needed frequently.

# Contents

# Glossary*

Contrary to traditional practice, the glossary of terms required for this monograph is placed before the text rather than after, to emphasize its importance in what intends to be a definitive study. The definitions given are those of the author. Their purpose is only to assist the reader in knowing the sense in which key words are being used and therefore they have been kept as brief as possible.

Page numbers indicate where a use or further discussion of a term may be found.

*Adaptivity*: Capability of an instructional system to adjust to the specific needs of the individual learner.

*Application*: A specific instance of a general use (see *use*).

*Audiovisual (A-V)*: Concerning both hearing and vision.

*Bandwidth*: The difference in frequency between the maximum and minimum boundaries of a telecommunication channel.

*Broadcast*: Transmitted via the public radio or television channels on a broad or nondirectional beam (see *open-circuit*) and received on generally available apparatus.

*Some of the definitions are based on entries in *Webster's Seventh New Collegiate Dictionary*, G. & C. Merriam Co., Springfield, Mass., 1967; some others have been adapted from English and English, *A Comprehensive Dictionary of Psychological and Psychoanalytical Terms*, Longmans, Green and Co., New York, 1958.

*Cartridge*: A device that contains and protects a film or tape during storage and playback and obviates the necessity for threading the playback magazine. In some cases the material is also recorded upon while it is within the cartridge. A cartridge generally contains only one program unit (see *magazine*). (92, 94)

*Cathode-ray tube (CRT)*: One of several types of vacuum tubes used generally for display purposes (e.g., TV picture tubes, oscilloscope display tubes, computer graphic displays, etc.). (81)

*Closed-circuit*: Any transmission method by which reception is not available to the general public. It may be confined to wires, microwave beams, and the like, or it may require special receiving apparatus not generally available. (89)

*Communication*: The sending and receiving of messages. (17)

*Communication aids*: Devices and materials that assist a communicator in expressing his message (see *instructional aids*). (6)

*Communication medium*: A system for conveying messages through reproducible and self-contained programs (see *instructional medium*). (6)

*Computer assisted instruction*: Applications of computers to the many aspects of the instructional process. (80-85)

*Constructed response*: Any response which is not finally effected by choosing one of two or more possible choices (see *selected response*). Examples are spoken or written words or phrases, drawings, and performance of actions and procedures.

*Criterion objective*: A major point in a course curriculum, essential to mastery of the course itself.

*Cross-Media*: Multimedia. (69-76)

*Electron Beam Recording (EBR)* (trade name): A method of recording television signals on motion-picture film by scanning the film with an electron beam rather than by focusing an image upon it. (97-98)

*Electronic Video Recording (EVR)* (trade name): A motion-picture system by means of which two tracks of picture and magnetic sound are recorded by electron beam on a film 8.75mm wide. (98-99)

*Enabling objective*: A minor point in a course curriculum, necessary to the mastery of a major objective (see *criterion objectives*).

*Facsimile*: A transmission-recording system in which pictures or print are transformed into electrical signals, in the manner of television, except very much more slowly and thus needing a very much narrower bandwidth for transmission. The output of the system is hard copy. (123-124)

*Filmstrip*: A communication medium involving static graphic materials which are recorded on a roll, usually of standard sprocketed motion-picture film, and projected frame-by-frame for group viewing. (127-128)

*Frame*: (1) A single still-picture isolated from a sequence of still-pictures, in still-visual or motion-visual media; (2) a discrete increment of information presented to a learner by an instructional program.

*Full motion*: Any kind of motion except "build-up" or "pointing."

*Hard copy*: Printed material of any kind ordinarily read by the unaided eye.

*Hardware*: Equipment as distinguished from materials; machinery, tools, and devices (see *software*).

*Independent-access*: A term that applies to a multiuser storage system in which the method and time required for any one user to gain access to a piece of information are apparently independent of the number of and actions of all other users (see *random-access, sequential-access*). (111)

*Individual mode*: One person alone, using materials at will, with control over the materials to a lesser or greater extent and limited interaction with other users. (43)

*Information*: (a) Statements in language on abstract subjects (conveying concepts, relationships, values, etc.); (b) percepts or observations of concrete subjects: physical properties, actions, conditions, changes, and the like; (c) combinations of (a) and (b), e.g., audiovisual information presentation. (9-10, 11-12)

*Information medium*: A system for transmitting, or for recording, storing, and retrieving information. (11-12)

*Instruction*: Teaching and learning; the systematic attempt to impart knowledge and skills, and to instigate learning. (10-11, 12-13)

*Instructional aids*: Communication aids used by an instructor generally in the presentation of information. They are not self-supporting. Many *"audiovisual aids"* are really *communication media,* since they can be self-supporting (see *learner aids*). (41-43)

*Instructional devices*: Training devices; items of standard on-the-job equipment used in instruction (see *instructional aids, learner aids*).

*Instructional medium*: Any component of the learning environment which provides or helps to provide stimuli to learning (see *communication medium* for distinction).

*Instructional method*: A structured activity for achieving learning.

*Instructional program*: (1) The information presentation component of a lesson (e.g., an instructional television program); (2) a lesson or other segment of *programmed instruction* which presents information in small increments, elicits learner response, and provides the learner with knowledge of results. (14, 15)

*Instructional technology*: Tools, materials, devices, machines and the procedures of their systematic use to achieve learning.

*Instructional television (ITV)*: Any audio-motion-visual system, using teletransmission, that is used primarily for formal instruction. (47-51)

*Instructional Television Fixed Service (ITFS)*: A television wireless transmission/reception system utilizing special frequencies which are allocated for instructional transmission purposes only, such as between a central transmitter and several school buildings. ITFS may be used in an educational system for administrative communication, data transmission, studio-transmitter links, and interstation relay.

*Interaction*: Mutual or reciprocal action or influence.

*Kinescope recording (kinerecording)*: A system for recording television sound and image on photographic film. Basically, it consists of a film camera focused on a kinescope tube (television picture tube). An ordinary motion-picture film results, which can be projected on a screen or transmitted by television in the normal manner. (95-97)

*Knowledge*: The body of integrated and retrievable information possessed by an individual. (10-11)

*Learner aids*: Devices that aid a learner, generally in drill and practice activities, with or without the assistance of an instructor. The learner uses or interacts directly with the device. Includes tools such as pencil and paper, and simulators for individual or team practice.

*Light pen*: Input device for a computer system; a stylus whose position when held against the face of a CRT can be determined by the computer. (82)

*Line graphics*: Charts, diagrams, maps, and drawings which do not attempt realism. (68)

*Live*: In real-time; that is, the message originates simultaneously or nearly simultaneously with its display and perception. (31-34)

*Magazine*: An adjunct to a projector or other playback device holding a set of program materials consisting of many individual units and generally accessed automatically, e.g., a slide magazine (see *cartridge*).

*Mass Medium*: A telemedium or recording medium which generally involves a large number of message receivers per sender and generally does not involve simultaneous interaction. It is available to the general public.

*Medium* pl. *media*: A means of effecting or conveying something. *Medium* is a general term roughly comparable in many ways with tool, instrument, vehicle, means, etc. (see *communication medium*). (5)

*Message*: An organized amount of information which has been formulated by one person with the intent of its immediate or ultimate transmission to other persons (or to himself), e.g., statements, questions, or commands. (36)

*Microfiche*: A microform system using transparent chips (cards), usually 4 x 6 inches in size, onto which up to 3200 pages of printed material may be photographically recorded. Can be read with magnifying or projection devices (see *ultramicroform*). (129-131)

*Microfilm*: A microform system using roll film on which photographic images of printed materials, usually, are reproduced. Can be read with magnifying or projection devices. (129-131)

*Microform*: Any recorded image of printed materials in which the reduction ratio is at least 12 to 1, usually 20 to 1 or greater. (129-131)

*Mode*: (1) (General). Manner of being, doing, etc. ; way; method. (2) Manner of reception of a communication, e.g., individual or group mode. (3) Manner of operation of equipment, e.g., recording or playback mode. (4) Manner of utilizing the possible ways of representing information via a medium, e.g., full or partial modes of use.

*Multi-image (Multimage)*: Two or more images, still or motion, projected as one display.

*Multimedia*: More than one medium used in a single communication, either sequentially or simultaneously. (69-76)

*Network*: (1) Telemedia: A series of reception, display, or redistribution points that are interconnected so they may simultaneously share the same programs. (2) Recording media: A series of points as in (1) above that share programs by transporting recordings between them. (3) Various combinations of (1) and (2).

*Open-circuit*: A broadcast transmission method in which the receiving equipment and programs are available to the general public. Open-circuit programs usually can be, with the necessary equipment, received anywhere. ITFS transmissions, by contrast, are not open-circuit.

*Picturephone* (trade name): A system of transmitting video and audio information via a relatively narrow bandwidth, involving digital encoding. Intended as a two-way system to enhance telephone intercommunication. (89-91)

*Practicable*: Something that can easily or readily be effected by available means or under current conditions.

*Print*: A way of representing information using symbols such as alphanumeric characters, pictographs, logograms, ideograms, hieroglyphics, and handwriting. Does not include line graphics or pictures. (67-68)

*Production*: Encoding of a message into the form of a program appropriate to the medium being used; the process of creating programs. May include such phases as program planning, preparation, script writing, rehearsal, and recording and/or live transmission. May also include testing, revision, and validation. (19, 32)

*Program*: (1) Any prearranged plan or course of proceedings; an organized sequence of events. (2) A unified presentation occupying a discrete period of time and having a beginning, a middle, and an end. *Program* is a general term covering entertainment, fine art, general interest, and instruction. Program as used here refers to the content of a medium, and consists generally of a message expressed in the terms and techniques of the medium (see also *instructional program*). (36-41)

*Radiovision*: An instructional media system presenting static visual materials and sound. The sound portion is transmitted by radio, while visual materials are projected at the point of local reception. (136-37)

*Random-access*: Direct-access. A method of storage in which any unit of information may be assessed directly, regardless of the location of the previous piece of information retrieved. An example would be the type of slide projector in which any slide could be projected promptly by pressing a corresponding button (see *independent-access, sequential-access*).

*Rand Tablet*: An input device for computer system consisting of a printed-circuit surface electrostatically coupled to a stylus. The computer senses the position of the stylus and thus makes possible the input of two-dimensional line drawings. (82)

*Recording media*: Media capable of recording programs, storing them, then playing them back at later times or, after transportation, at later times *and* at different places. (20-23)

*Selected response*: A response which is finally effected by choosing the best answer from two or more possibilities which have been prepared for the learner and presented to him. Selections may be made by pencil on paper, keyboard, light pen or the like (see *constructed response*).

*Self-instruction*: Independent study structured and carried out by the learner himself and performed in the individual mode. Self-instruction may incorporate heuristic methods such as inquiry, search, and discovery. (15)

*Self-study*: Individual study. Any learning activity carried on by the learner that is not coordinated with other persons. (15)

*Sequential-access*: A method of storage in which the items of information stored become available in a one-after-the-other sequence, whether all the information or only some of it is desired. An example would be a normal slide projector, in which a desired slide can be projected immediately only if it happens to be next in sequence (see *independent-access, random-access*).

*Slide-set*: A set of slides, usually contained in a magazine, for projection in an automatic projector. (129)

*Slow-scan television*: A transmission system which transmits still-pictures in near real-time, generally at a rate of six or fewer frames per minute, to be displayed on a CRT; a communication medium based on slow-scan transmission. (106-108)

*Software*: (1) Telemedia: Transmitted programs and/or messages. (2) Recording media: Recorded program materials, e.g., film, tapes, books, discs, etc., containing recorded messages. (3) Both: Working materials from which a program is created. May include scripts, written narration, audio or visual aids, etc., especially created or assembled for the production.

*Sound-on-slide*: An instructional media system involving slides mounted in special holders or cartridges that include up to a minute of magnetic recording material, so that sound may be recorded "onto the slide itself" and played back from the slide during projection. (115-116)

*Sound page*: An instructional media system involving separate pages of hard copy with sound recorded on the back of each page. The page is placed on the top of a record/reproduce machine; the learner views the page and hears the sound. (116)

*Subsidiary Communications Authorization (SCA)*: A broadcasting system which makes it possible to transmit up to five simultaneous programs on a single FM radio channel. One of these is the main channel, the others are multiplexed subchannels (subcarriers). (135)

*Teaching*: The art of assisting or instigating another to learn; it includes the presentation of information and the providing of appropriate situations, directions, or activities designed to facilitate learning.

*Telecommunication media (telemedia)*: Electronic media capable of transmitting programs across distance in real-time. (6)

*Telelecture*: An instructional media system involving the use of static visuals and sound. The sound portion is transmitted by telephone while the synchronized visual materials are projected at the point of local reception. Since standard telephone facilities are used, a feedback channel is also available. (133)

*Telewritevision*: An instructional media system incorporating telewriting plus static visual materials projected by the telewriting display equipment at the point of viewing. (118-119)

*Telewriting*: An instructional media system which transmits sound and writing as it is being written. The principle is basically that of the TelAutograph: The vertical and horizontal components of movement of the sending stylus are transferred to electrical impulses which are then transmitted on different channels to a receiving stylus which moves in accordance with the signals it receives, and reproduces, simultaneously, the original writing. This may then be projected on a screen for group viewing. (117-118)

*Terminal*: Interface equipment between user and machine in a computer system; input-output equipment, usually in the form of teletype and/or CRT. (81-83)

*Time-shared television*: A proposed transmission system which would utilize one television channel to transmit, for instance, 300 still-pictures to 300 different viewers each 10 seconds, instead of the usual 300 successive frames of a single moving picture. (108-109)

*Transmission*: An electrical or electromagnetic process whereby a properly encoded message may cross space to a decoding apparatus in real-time. (20)

*Ultramicroform*: Any microform in which the reduction ratio is greater than 40 to 1. (130)

*Use*: A manner of employing a communication medium, named for the general purpose or objective which it helps to attain. *Uses* are general and abstract; *applications* are specific and concrete (see also *application, utilization*).

*Utilization*: Use at the receiving end of a media system; *utilization* of communication in an instructional system refers to the manner in which an instructional program is integrated into the whole instructional system; that is, how it is coordinated with other instructional activities.

*Video recording file (VTR file)*: An information storage and retrieval system using video tape as the storage medium. (131-132)

*Video tape*: Thin (0.5 to 1.5 mil.) acetate or mylar tape of various widths (normally between 1/4 inch and 2 inches), coated with magnetic material, used to record and store video and audio information.

*A TAXONOMY OF COMMUNICATION MEDIA*

| TELECOMMUNICATION | Sound | Picture | Line Graphic | Print | Motion | RECORDING |
|---|---|---|---|---|---|---|
| CLASS I:  AUDIO-MOTION-VISUAL MEDIA | | | | | | |
|  | X | X | X | X | X | Sound film |
| Television | X | X | X | X | X | Video tape |
|  |  |  |  |  |  | Film TV recording |
|  | X | X | X | X | X | Holographic recording |
| Picturephone | X | X | X | X | X |  |
| CLASS II:  AUDIO-STILL-VISUAL MEDIA | | | | | | |
| Slow-scan TV  Time-shared TV | X | X | X | X |  | Recorded still TV |
|  | X | X | X | X |  | Sound filmstrip |
|  | X | X | X | X |  | Sound slide-set |
|  | X | X | X | X |  | Sound-on-slide |
|  | X | X | X | X |  | Sound page |
|  | X | X | X | X |  | Talking book |
| CLASS III:  AUDIO-SEMIMOTION MEDIA | | | | | | |
| Telewriting | X |  | X | X | × | Recorded telewriting |
| CLASS IV:  MOTION-VISUAL MEDIA | | | | | | |
|  |  | X | X | X | X | Silent film |
| CLASS V:  STILL-VISUAL MEDIA | | | | | | |
| Facsimile |  | X | X | X |  | Printed page |
|  |  | X | X | X |  | Filmstrip |
|  |  | X | X | X |  | Picture set |
|  |  | X | X | X |  | Microform |
|  |  | X | X | X |  | Video file |
| CLASS VI:  AUDIO MEDIA | | | | | | |
| Telephone  Radio | X |  |  |  |  | Audio disc  Audio tape |
| CLASS VII:  PRINT MEDIA | | | | | | |
| Teletype |  |  |  | X |  | Punched paper tape |

The Communication Media

# 1.

# Introduction

This monograph, the first of a proposed series of writings on the subject of communication media, is intended to be definitive and descriptive, and, hopefully, currently complete. Much has been written about "new media" and "newer media." There has been much viewing with hope, as well as viewing with alarm. To date, however, there exists no exhaustive list of all these media, both new and old, with a comparison of their characteristics and an analysis of the various alternatives for the media user to consider. An attempt has been made to provide such a classified listing; it is presented here as the frontispiece of this volume.

The term "medium" has many definitions, from a solution for mixing paints to a person who purports to make contact with the dear departed. In all of its meanings, however, a medium is something in the middle, between other things, and most often it is considered as a vehicle or instrument for making something happen. In instruction or in advertising, to mention two common examples of systems which use communication, media include all the different kinds of methods and devices that these systems use to achieve their disparate ends. This very broad meaning for medium is narrowed, however, when the word "communication" is added. *Communication media* are specific kinds of systems, the capabilities of which are so vastly different from those of mere tools, aids, or vehicles for communication, that they deserve to be separately studied and analyzed.

Communication media have frequently been confused in many people's thinking with communication *aids,* particularly in instruction. This is because they have traditionally been administered by school audiovisual people along with various other kinds of learning resources and instructional aids for the classroom teacher. An important distinction is made in this monograph between media that are merely instructional aids and media that are communication systems. Basically, an aid merely supports a teacher's presentation, whereas a communication medium is self-supporting. A communication medium, within its specific limits, is capable of the entirety of information presentation and of instigating learner/subject matter interaction. Moreover, communication media programs can be widely reproducible. While communication media cannot take over all the functions now performed by a good classroom teacher, they have enormous potential for increasing both the quality and quantity of available education.

The term "communication media" is commonly erroneously understood to include only "*tele*communication" media, those media which electronically transmit information in real time, and to exclude media which record and store. This monograph will discuss recording media as well as telemedia, both of which will be subsumed under the term "communication media."

Perhaps because of the lack of analysis of communication media and what they can do, many possible uses of the more simple, inexpensive media were not conceived until complex, expensive media such as television and film had been applied to these uses. It will sometimes be pointed out that one application of television, for instance, does not require real-time transmission, and another application does not require pictures in motion; therefore, much of what instructional TV is doing could be done as well by less expensive means such as still TV, telewriting, filmstrips, or even radio. Thus, there is a growing tendency on the part of media users to investigate possible alternative systems among the minor media.

In the discussion of communication media as systems, it will be shown how they participate as subsystems in the functioning of larger "user" systems such as instruction, advertising, political propaganda, and the like. Because of the particular importance of instruction, and the current very high interest in the application of communication media to instructional purposes, most of the examples which are given to illustrate uses of these media will be chosen from the instructional field. Closely associated with instruction is the field of information organization, storage and retrieval. Communication media play an important role in information systems, too, and may serve both functions simultaneously when individuals are involved in information retrieval for self-instructional purposes.

A distinction will first be made between information and instruction, recognizing that a few of the communication media are indeed used primarily for the storage or transmission of isolated or improvised information (e.g., the microform media, the telephone, and punched paper tape) rather than what we shall define later as programs. Beyond this point, information systems, which have been the subject of many excellent studies and are well understood, will not be an important referent in this report.

The criteria which have been used for distinguishing a communication medium from a communication aid will be presented, as well as criteria for distinguishing between one medium and another, and for distinguishing between a single medium and a multimedia application.

Finally, each of the communication media which have been identified and listed will be briefly described and discussed. A number of proposed new media which are not yet in general use will also be included.

The philosophy behind much of this analysis of communication systems is a functional approach which sees existence as a great, interacting series of systems within systems. Every whole is but a part of something which is greater, itself only part of something greater yet. In the physical world the known series of systems extends from the universe down to the systems we call atoms. Social systems can be seen as similarly related, extending from the individual on out possibly to all mankind. This monograph is not the place for a full presentation of this epistemology; the reader is simply asked to go along with the functional approach, as far as he can, with the promise that it will be useful in understanding the nature of communication media as they are analyzed in this monograph. Arthur Koestler in *The Ghost in the Machine* visualizes a Janus god, looking in two directions, representing the "holon"—the whole that is also a part of a larger whole. The author replaces Koestler's holons with "systems," and conceives of these entities as contained one within the other, interacting often in very complex ways, forming networks of interaction which may themselves be systems, each with some sort of output or purpose.

# 2.

# Information
# and Instruction

In any discussion of communication media we must use the terms "information" and "instruction." It is important that these terms be clearly defined, and the distinction between them made clear. The word "knowledge" must also be defined, since the interaction between what is meant by knowledge and what we are calling instruction and information is an important determinant to some of these meanings. The definitions used here are based partly on dictionary definitions, partly on a feel for frequency and generality of current use, and partly on their usefulness to the kinds of thinking needed in this area.

Any organism with sensory perception of any kind receives information from its environment. From the simplest phototropic animal responding to the presence of light, to the multisensory perception of man, organisms are constantly receiving information. Information can be broadly defined as that which is perceived. When I see or smell smoke, I am informed that something may be on fire. When I touch and lift an object I receive much information about its density of mass, its conductance of heat, its surface texture, its compressibility, and so forth. When we talk about information in terms of information *systems,* however, information transmission, storage, retrieval and the like, we are using the word in a more restricted sense. Of course this kind of information must be perceived, but it must also be *sent.* Information, in this sense, is the content of a message and is originated by a *message sender.* We might refer to it as human or artificial information to distinguish it from perceptions originating in the natural environment. The best term to use, however, is "message." The use of the term "message" connotes information which comes from a message sender intended for a message receiver. The sender may be machine as well as man; the receiver may be man, or a machine equipped with sensing devices.

The simplest message is the statement.* A statement, like a sentence, contains subject, verb, and predicate, either expressed or implied. The telephone directory is filled with information like "John Smith: 467-2772" implying the full statement, "John Smith's phone number is 467-2772." Any datum of any kind is a statement, even though some of the statement is only implied, as in the telephone listing, or supplied by context as in the case of a one-word answer to a question. Just the name "John Smith," in total isolation, would be no information to anyone. Thus information, in the sense in which it is used when referring to human information systems, and the sense in which it is used here, can be defined as the content of messages. This is a continuum running from the simplest statement to the most complex sequence of related statements or simultaneously presented cues, generally represented in sound, print, line graphic, picture, motion or in some combination of these modes.

Instruction, unlike information, is not a *thing* which can exist in space or time, but a *process,* in the sense of "a series of actions or operations conducing to an end."[1]

We will think of knowledge as something that is stored or filed in the brain. Specific information, concepts, relationships, and so forth, must be sensed, perceived, comprehended and then integrated into the learner's existing structure of associations in

---

*declarative, interrogative, imperative, etc.

order to become knowledge. Knowledge, in short, is the content of human memory organized for retrieval. This organization is sometimes referred to as knowledge structure. All knowledge is transitory, to some degree, but any knowledge can be retained longer than unassociated information.

Information systems and instructional systems both use communication as a component (or subsystem) functioning in coordination with other subsystems. In both cases these communication systems carry messages, the content of which is information. The difference is in purpose. The purpose of the instructional system is achieving learning in a *learner*; the purpose of the information system is informing an information *user*. An information system may indeed be part of an instructional system, but can play only a limited role in the instructional process. Merely informing someone does not necessarily affect his file of knowledge.

Although a person may add the information he receives to his knowledge, the mere delivery of information is not designed and directed toward this end, as instruction is. The information user generally has a task at hand which he is interested in resolving; he acquires information, uses it in his task, and may forget it quickly—if he ever retains it at all. Information systems are designed for *use* and for the convenience of the user. Instructional systems are designed to achieve *learning*—to affect the knowledge of the learner.

## INFORMATION

Information has far less structure than knowledge; much information, in fact, consists of isolated and unrelated facts. In general, unrelated information can be filed in a human memory only when it has become associated with some prior structure of understanding and has become part of a person's knowledge.

In the design of information systems, we are concerned with information outside the individual: the technology of information-handling; the systems of processing, storage and retrieval; and the physical means of conveying and imparting information to others. Because information so often consists of isolated data, to be useful it must be filed within various classifications, often alphabetical, so that it can be retrieved. Thus we have directories, bibliographies and statistical tables of many kinds. Considerable predigestion of information is done by librarians, who, for example, prepare annotated bibliographies, which add a dimension of qualitative evaluation to what would otherwise be unevaluated information.*

The librarian may serve the instructor by assisting him in the preparation of information for use in the instructional process; the librarian may indeed serve the learner directly, in his capacity as a user. The learner himself then may take the information retrieved and build it into his knowledge. It has been said that there is no teaching, there is only learning; however, well-designed instruction can greatly facilitate the learning process. It is rare that a librarian plays the part of instructor, mainly because the instructional process involves so much more than the mere presentation of information.

## INSTRUCTION

The role of information in the instructional process occurs primarily in the lesson-presentation phase, and when the learning objectives are mainly cognitive. However, since instruction includes much more than the mere presentation of information, it will contain, or be based on, a strategy for achieving the desired learning. The instructional process may include stimuli designed to elicit thought or overt action, or to stimulate discussion among

---

*Future librarians may go much further. Information needs to be directly available within its sources (books, journals, etc.) or extracted from its sources so it can be directly addressable. Further, there is a need for search and retrieval systems in which indexing is associative.

two or more learners; it may, if properly programmed, be so systematized that the learner cannot obtain access to one piece of the contained information until he has demonstrated by some action that he has apprehended the preceding and prerequisite information.

One of the important objectives of good instruction is to give the learner the skills required to seek out information on his own, and to devise activities which will help him to use and retain that information. Most important of all, instruction should contain an intrinsic element of motivation and encouragement to capture, hold and increase the learner's interest and his desire to know. None of this strategy plays any role at all in simple information retrieval by a user with an immediate task at hand.

## AN INFORMATION–INSTRUCTION MODEL

Figure 1 presents a model of the processes of information retrieval and instruction. The large block labeled "information" represents the recorded information of the world. The input to this vast data bank is shown at the bottom, where reality is observed and becomes known facts—hence data. The librarian, knowing the needs of various kinds of users, works within this area, creating and maintaining order. All recorded information and all of the order it may possess exists ostensibly for one reason only: so that this information may be imparted to others.*

Probably most information is arranged for the convenience of the information user, shown at the upper left. He receives the information, uses it in performing his task, and usually then loses

---

*It is also recognized that a vast quantity of academic information comes into existence so that whole documents can be traded as unit commodities for professional advancement and the like; the merit of their detailed contents is a secondary consideration. In these cases, there is serious doubt whether they should be called messages at all. Although expressed in the message form, they really are not communications. Like "art for art's sake," they are objects and that is all.

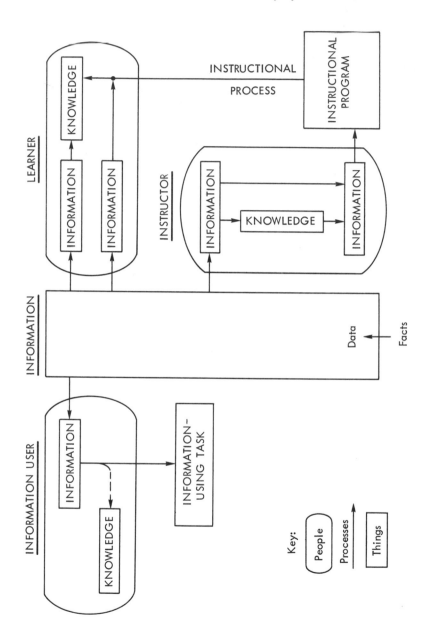

*Figure 1.* Conceptual model of information and instruction relationships.

or buries it. The person with a photographic memory is a rare exception.

Information is also retrieved by the instructor, shown at the lower right, whose purpose is to build it into instruction. Most of this information enters his knowledge, where it is combined with existing knowledge acquired from experience or earlier training. Out of this combined knowledge a selection of information is made, organized and encoded as an instructional message. Some of the information which the instructor retrieves, however, may not actually go into his knowledge bank at all, but may be used directly in his instructional task. (This is represented by the arrow bypassing the instructor's knowledge.) The amount of information taking this route will vary inversely with the creativity of the instructor.

That part of the instructional process which contains information—the lesson—is labeled "Instructional Program" in Figure 1. The reason is this: the term "instructional program," originating in the vocabulary of programmed instruction, implies considerably more than the presentation of information; it also includes the direction of learner activities relevant to the information, the provision of resources, and the application of methods for the practice of responses until the achievement of stated learning objectives can be certified. Thus it may encompass some, much, or all of the instructional process. The program may actually direct the entire process, then, rather than simply initiate it, as the lesson commonly does.

As stated above, one of the most important objectives of instruction, especially in terms of lifelong education, is to train the learner to utilize the information bank directly and to devise his own instructional process. This skill should be called self-instruction or independent study rather than self-study, since with it, the learner directs his own activities. "Self-study" describes any learning activity of any sort which is performed individually, even if it is no more than rote memorization. Self-instruction, on the other hand, incorporates heuristic methods such as inquiry and search-and-discovery. The lower arrow from the information bank to the learner represents the activities involved in learning self-instructional skills. The upper arrow represents this same process taking place outside the instructional process after transfer of the learned heuristic skills, so to speak, into daily life.

During this process, the learner may be considered in much the same light as the information user, except that his task at hand is not external—it is the acquiring of knowledge. Students, especially college students, may play the part of the mere information user, and this is encouraged by a limited concept on the part of many people, i.e., that instruction is merely the process of dishing out information. The task at hand for the student is often a paper or an examination on which he hopes to get a good grade. Cramming for an exam is a kind of information-using; the crammer is frequently not really interested in retention beyond a few hours or days, at the most.

A commonly held view is that learning is achieved only when information has been related to an individual's store of patterns and structures; that is, when it has become knowledge. Such knowledge then becomes part of the way the learner views the world, and it helps determine the manner in which he perceives reality. Information that is not so related finds no structure in which to be filed, which may explain why it is not long retained.

# 3.

# What Are
# Communication Media?

*THE COMMUNICATION PROCESS*

Reduced to its simplest form, communication is a three-step process for the dynamic transfer of information from one person to another. The process of communication by human speech, for instance, may be traced as follows:

1. A message sender selects a thought from his knowledge formulated in words, so that it exists separate from his knowledge ready to be transmitted.
2. When he speaks, he sends forth his message, encoded in spoken words which travel as vibrations in the medium of the air.
3. These sounds are perceived by a message-receiver, filtered out from the noise that accompanies them, and if the language is known to the receiver, decoded and comprehended. If the information is considered valuable enough, it may immediately be "filed" as knowledge.

The original thought may go through inadvertent changes

during any of the phases of the process, especially the first and last phases, when it is emerging from and merging into knowledge. The message may become distorted during transmission or become obscured by noise. In any case, during the entire process of communication, knowledge exists as information both inside and outside an individual. When information is transmitted, or recorded, it becomes what we call a message.

Before the message is sent, the information involved reposes as knowledge in the sender's mind, most probably in largely verbal form. With the sending of the message this information is organized by the sender into a more or less complex structure with the purpose of imparting the information, immediately or eventually, to one or more receivers.

For communication in the face-to-face situation, simple transmission by sound or light (or other direct perceptual means) is all that is required. When distance or time is to be covered, the message must be carried by a communication medium.

The speech example did not include the use of a communication medium; the medium of air is only a medium of transmission, not of communication. The simplest communication medium first entered the human scene when a messenger was utilized to convey the message to a distant place. Because of the unreliability of human memory, communication advanced another stage when the runner was given a knotted string and later a written scroll to carry. The recording of words as written language did not change the essential nature of the message as information in transit. The storage of the message in written form, even for years, is only a delay stage in the general process of transit. All messages—spoken, signalled, transmitted, recorded, stored, or transported—are in transit from the time they are first encoded and sent until they are received by the last person whom they may concern. Thus we must realize that systems that record and store information are communication media just as much as systems which transmit information in real time. Figure 2 is a simplified model of the communication process, showing the role that a communication medium may play in assisting the transmission of a message.

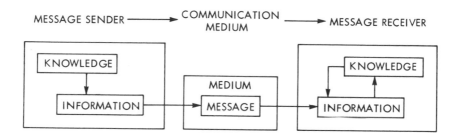

*Figure 2.* Simplified conceptual model of the communication process.

## THE COMMUNICATION MEDIUM AS A SYSTEM

A communication medium, like any other system, has inputs, processes and outputs, coordinating with various other systems in constantly changing and frequently overlapping patterns. It is composed of subsystems, each of which can be thought of as a whole system in itself.

The prime input to the communication system is the message, which has been conceived and formulated by some message sender and fed into the medium. Other inputs include manpower, materials, facilities and the like. The prime output is the message, which is displayed for the attention of the desired message receiver.

The three major parts of a telecommunication medium are: (1) the program production subsystem, (2) the transmission subsystem, and (3) the program display subsystem. Within each of these systems, such as the program production subsystem for instance, there may be further subsystems such as: (a) a program writing and visualizing system, (b) a program materials generation system, (c) a studio rehearsal and production system, (d) a program editing system, and so forth.

A communication system that is a recording medium, such as film or video tape, rather than a telecommunication medium like live television, includes a recording-storing-reproducing system (*recording system* for short) instead of a transmission system.

In Figure 3, Part (a) diagrams a typical transmission system and Part (b) shows the role it plays in a *tele*communication system. Part (c) diagrams a recording system and (d) shows the role it plays in the *recorded* communication system.

## COMMUNICATION *Versus* TRANSMISSION OR RECORDING

The full communication system is frequently confused with its transmission or recording component, especially since both are commonly referred to by the same name. Thus, the word "television" may be used to mean merely a means of transmitting picture and sound (a *transmitting* medium) or it may mean a means of communicating via picture and sound. Used in the latter sense, it must of course include means for the generation of programs and environment for the perception of programs. Only in this sense does the word television refer to a telecommunication medium.

Many kinds of wired or wireless transmitting circuits are each capable of carrying program software associated with several different communication media; for example, telephone lines may carry teletype or telewriting communications and radio programs as well as telephone conversations. Not all communication media are also transmitting media, and there are many transmitting media, such as laser beams, wave guides, and the like, that are not at present considered to be communication media. A transmission medium does not include any program software; in the example of television, again, it need not even include cameras and microphones at one end of the system, or display equipment at the other end.

It is characteristic of the television transmitting system, for instance, that it can theoretically transmit almost anything that can be recorded, whatever combination of sound, picture, or print it may contain. In such a case *it is the recording system which should be considered the communication medium, not the transmitting system, because the recording system contains the program software elements.* When a film is transmitted by television, for instance, film is the communication medium; television is only the transmitting medium. It is only when the program is specifically made for the television transmission system that the whole may be termed a television communication medium. If the television program is prerecorded on video tape and subsequently broadcast, it is correct to say that *video tape* is the communication medium; television again is only a system for transmission.

The same confusion occurs between mere recording systems and the communication media that are based on these recording systems. The magnetic-tape recording system, for instance, is only a recording medium. Magnetic-tape recording systems may be used to record audio, video, telewriting, or slow-scan TV. They contain only recording equipment, recording material (tape), and playback equipment. Neither a video tape *recording* system nor a television *transmission* system need include cameras and microphones at one end of the system, or display equipment at the other. Neither of these will include program materials.

In addition to a transmitting system, the *telecommunication* system, as shown in (b) of Figure 3, will incorporate components which concern the program. The same is true of the *recording communication* system (d). Program origination (planning and production) and program display (making the program visible and/or audible) are part of neither transmitting nor recording processes, yet are vital parts of the communication system.

The purpose of a *transmission* system is simply to get a program from here to there. A *recording* system may have the same object, but in addition it bridges time, sending a program from now to then, with a minimum of loss, distortion, or added noise. Although those who believe that a tree falling on a deserted island makes no sound might disagree, the transmission system may function perfectly whether the program is actually displayed

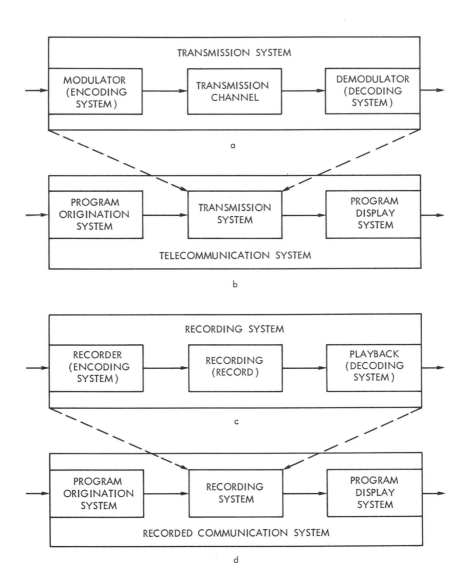

*Figure 3.* A transmission system (a) and the telecommunication system (b) that incorporates it; a recording system (c) and the recorded communication system (d) that incorporates it.

for anyone or not. Successful or effective transmission is independent of what sort of programs are sent, i.e., what kind of communications are achieved by the communication system of which it is a part. Communication, in turn, can function as a complete system whether or not anyone actually views the displayed program. A successful or effective communication system is also independent of the messages its programs may contain, how the messages may affect their recipients, or whether the results are good or bad.


## THE COMMUNICATION MEDIUM AS A SUBSYSTEM

The communication medium, while it is a system complete within itself, is always, if it is productive of anything at all, part of a larger system which we may call the "user system." In our discussion of the communication medium as a system we have not used the terms "sender" or "receiver" because both of these essential elements of the communication *process* are outside the communication *medium.* Both the sender and the receiver of a message are part of the user system; the sender generates the message as *input* to the communication system, the receiver perceives and comprehends the message *output.* The message passes through the communication system, so to speak, in at one end, out at the other, leaving the system without a message anymore, waiting to be used again. In the process the managers of the communication system do their best to enhance the message with good program organization and technique, and to avoid covering it up or distracting from it with irrelevant stimuli.

The user system, which includes sender and receiver, may have any of a variety of purposes. It may be an instructional system, in which the sender is generally an instructor or instructional team, and the receiver is a learner. It may be an advertising system, as in commercial radio and television, in which the message sender may be a manufacturer or distributor, and the receiver a consumer. It may be a public relations system, a public health system, a public information system, political system, or an art and entertainment system.

The user system gives meaning and value to the communication system. It always involves people directly or indirectly in its processes, who generate and dispatch messages back and forth. A communication system that is incorporated into a user system will be valued as useful in proportion to its contribution toward the successful functioning of the user system. Some systems are required simply to transmit or to store and retrieve *data*, without any requirement to build it into a program. These are the purely information systems; they include such media as microforms, video tape file, teletype and its recorded counterpart, punched paper tape—in most (but not all) of their applications.

Some user systems require communication media to turn out a product which is saleable for immediate use or enjoyment, and to be paid for by the receiver, either directly or indirectly; for example, in book publishing, in tax-supported broadcasting systems, or in pay-television. Typical of these are the art-entertainment systems (for this purpose art and entertainment are viewed as two ends of a continuum).

Some user systems have the aim of either temporarily or permanently affecting receiver behavior, and utilize communication media as one of several coordinated means of bringing this about. This category includes instructional systems and persuasion systems (such as advertising or political propaganda systems).

When a communication medium is incorporated into an instructional system, it is fed instructional messages from which instructional effects and results are expected. When a communication medium is used as part of an information system, or a propaganda system, or an entertainment system, its messages and its effects and results will be quite different, while the medium itself remains essentially the same.

The same film medium, for example, the identical cameras, laboratory equipment, film emulsions and projection equipment, the same trained operators, the same cameramen and projectionists, may be used in making and displaying instructional films, or commercials, or feature films, or other types of films, each of which has a different set of purposes. The output of the system we call the film medium is a moving image on a screen, or multiplicity of screens in many places at many times. Any results or effects of these screenings are part of the instructional, advertising, or entertainment system which uses the communication medium, and are outside and beyond the medium of film.

This explains why advocates of the use of communication media in education will foresee and claim benefits to be achieved *with the aid* of film or television, for instance, while being very careful not to state that film or television is expected to achieve these benefits by itself. There is a widespread misunderstanding here on the part of the general public.

The only contact many laymen have with instructional television occurs when they tune their home receivers to pre-breakfast adult courses. Observing no integration with student activities or other instructional methods, the casual viewer may form an impression of learners doing nothing but watching television sets. This then colors his view of in-school uses of the media as well. Of course *participation* in a broadcast course will usually involve the learner in various activities beyond viewing (such as correspondence and supplementary reading).

Communication media, in and of themselves, are rather limited in achieving productive results. They may affect people briefly, but other activities are generally needed (such as perform-ance practice) to make such changes permanent. Thus communica-tion alone, in instruction, for instance, generally is not sufficient to achieve learning. The objective of the instructional system— learning—is a personal, intrinsic process which requires responsive activities by the learner. But it must begin with communication of stimuli, selected and organized to bring about learning. Figure 4 is a simplified model of an instructional system, showing some of the more important functions in the teaching-learning process. Eleven distinct uses of communication media are identified.

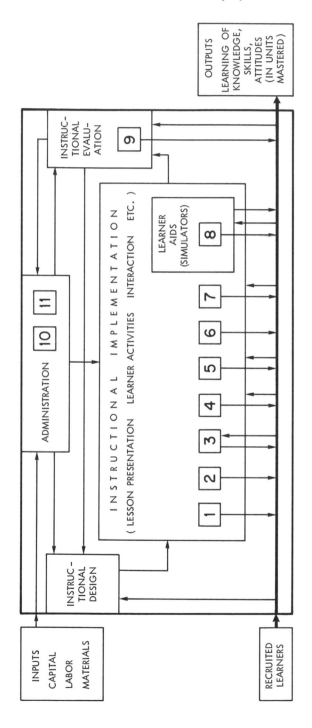

*Figure 4.* Diagram of a typical instructional system highly simplified. Various possible uses of communication media in instruction are shown in a logical order. However, they may be performed in many orders and many iterations. Often, several uses are served by a single program. If recruitment of learners is considered a part of the instructional system (it is an important part of some), a twelfth use may be listed.

1. *Knowledge of Learning Objectives.* Communication media are used to demonstrate to the learner the level of competence at which he can perform when he satisfactorily completes a given course of study.

2. *Motivation.* Media are used to persuade the learner to want to acquire the knowledge and skills which are about to be taught.

3. *Information Presentation.* Media are used to variously tell about, show, and enact the information which is the content of the instruction. Programming this presentation stimulates student response (up arrow).

4. *Stimulus for Discussion.* Media programs are used to stimulate thought and open a subject for discussion.

5. *Direction of Learner Activities.* Directions for assignments, demonstrations of techniques to be followed, step-by-step guidance in lab procedures.

6. *Control of Learner Activities (Drill and Practice).* Media can be patient and untiring drillmasters in providing stimuli to which the learner must practice responses.

7. *Reinforcement.* Media may ask the learner questions and offer encouragement, such as knowledge of correct results, which will increase the probability of his giving desired responses in the future.

8. *Simulation.* Media may be used as a component of various kinds of simulators, when the presentation of information is required.

9. *Evaluation.* When information is presented via a medium, it is appropriate to use the same medium in measuring learner achievement.

10. *Administration.* Many uses for communication lie in the purely administrative functions of managing instructional systems, outside the instructional curriculum.

11. *Research and Development.* Experimental projects often use media, whether they are testing or evaluating the effectiveness of the media themselves or using media to present identical stimuli to various subjects under various conditions.

Figures 3 and 4 place the communication media in proper perspective, which has not always been done in the past. The failure of much early educational broadcasting, for instance, stemmed from the broadcaster's involvement in communication *per se* and his failure to recognize the larger user system objectives which his medium may have been trying to help achieve. It is not sufficient to design, produce and transmit an educational program, even if it has been publicized sufficiently so that the intended audience is there to receive the broadcast. If the objective is learning, someone has to organize the learners—get them to commit themselves to action, follow up on the activities that the program may direct, provide human interaction and personal interest, and monitor, observe and measure their growth and achievement along the way. Mere lesson presentation is not the whole of instruction, just as communication is only a part of any user system.

## *THE AUTHORITATIVE Versus THE DEMOCRATIC\* HIERARCHIES*

Each system in a hierarchy of systems has its own manager, who may or may not know anything about the management of the systems which include or are included by his own. In general, the television transmitter engineer, who is manager of the encoding subsystem, is not capable of making the judgments required of the station's chief engineer, who is manager of the full transmission system. The chief engineer, in turn, is not capable of producing the program or managing the broadcast station. The station manager, in turn, is not capable of managing the overall marketing system, or educational system, which utilizes his program output.

*Used in Sense 4, Webster's Seventh New Collegiate Dictionary: "favoring social equality; not snobbish."

That a manager of a subsystem is not capable of operating the larger system within which he operates is not to say that he may not have some very good ideas or suggestions to make concerning the utilization of his system's output.

When a difference of opinion arises between a program producer and an engineer, for example, and there is equivalent competence, vision, intelligence, etc., on the part of the two persons involved, the producer is far more likely to be right. In authoritative hierarchies, such as military organizations, this high probability is crystallized into the authority of rank. The general, because he commands a division (a large system), must decide objectives the colonel's regiment (a subsystem) should achieve, and the colonel must then decide what the lieutenant colonel and captain under him should be doing with the smaller forces under their commands.

If the television engineer disagrees with what the producer is doing, and tells him so, he may be overstepping his authority. Courtsmartial for insubordination follow similar breaches of etiquette in the military. But the engineer may actually be right. In questioning the producer's judgment he is saying, in effect, I know more about the larger system that you manage, at least in this particular instance, than you do. The producer who realizes that this may indeed be true and utilizes without conflict suggestions coming from the manager of one of his subsystems will operate a more productive system than the producer who "pulls rank" and tries to pretend that his management cannot be improved upon by someone who does not have equal knowledge and competence.

It can be observed in practice that the manager of a superior system does not involve himself in the "housekeeping" details of *sub*system management except at the risk of lowering the effectiveness of both systems.

Generally in instructional television, and often in instructional films as well, the representative of the user system with whom the producer works is the very teacher who performs before the cameras. It is this teacher who has sat in at committee meetings to determine curriculum, who has planned the teacher's guide which suggests strategy for classroom utilization, and who has designed the instruction to be presented. Far from being merely "talent" to the producer, the TV teacher represents the management of the user system.

The instructional TV or film producer, however, very commonly patterns his relationships with his fellow workers after his own experience of his observation of relations in the entertainment field. The performer, in entertainment (if not always in fine art), is only one component of a production, along with script, music, settings and all the rest. When the commercial producer must bow to a representative of the system which uses his product, it is generally to an advertising agency man or sponsor.

The *authoritative* hierarchy assumes that no system manager has any competence beyond his own system. He is expected to "take orders" and accept the evaluations of his system which are made by its users. Bureaucrats like this kind of hierarchy because they are told what to do, and do not have to make decisions or take responsibility for innovation.

The *democratic* hierarchy assumes that the manager of a system knows something about the user system which he serves. He is thus capable of making useful suggestions as to how the output of his system could be better used. To the extent that his advice is sought and encouraged, he develops a better ability to evaluate his own system, since he can stand outside it, so to speak, taking the user system view.

The authoritative hierarchy appears to work best when a minimum of change to the system is desirable. The democratic hierarchy appears to be best when a growing, improving, changing system is desired, at, perhaps, the expense of short-term efficiency. In the case of communication media, few production systems turn out programs which are so ideally suited to the user's need that development, improvement and change are not at least as important as current efficiency. This is particularly true, of course, with instructional systems, but this fact is not always recognized.

Within a hierarchy of systems, when authority is needed it must flow from the larger system to the smaller. A manager of a subsystem should not have authority equal to or greater than that of the manager of the system within which he plays a part. Thus the manager of a communication system (or his representative, such as a TV program producer) should not have authority over the manager of an instructional system (or his representative, such as a television teacher). This is a relationship which has frequently been misunderstood.

This discussion could probably be summarized by saying that the engineer, technician, cameraman, or whoever the manager of the transmission or recording system may be, should work under the producer, production manager, executive program director, or whoever the manager of the communication system may be. The producer, for his part, should work under the manager of the user system. At the same time, each manager will develop a more productive system if he seeks advice from the managers of his subsystems.

## *TELEMEDIA AND RECORDING MEDIA*

Telecommunication media are those that can involve instantaneous transmission via wire, broadcast channel, or other such means. In the pure form of these media, origination of message or program is simultaneous with its reception. Setting aside for the moment the transmittal of previously recorded materials such as film on television, audio tapes on radio, etc., what one sees or hears through these media is being picked up by a microphone or scanned by a camera at the very moment of broadcast; the program exists in real time. The viewer or listener can experience immediacy, knowing that what he sees or hears is at that very

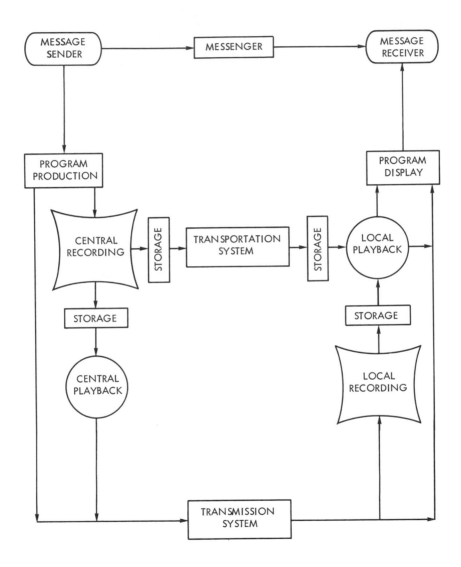

*Figure 5.* Conceptual model of telemedia and recording media integration.

moment happening in a distant place.* The possible advantages or importance of "seeing at a distance," right now, rather than seeing something which was recorded in the past, will be discussed later.

The media have been divided into seven classes based on the combinations of audio and visual elements which they utilize (see Table 1). The characteristics of these classes will be discussed in detail in a later section. The relationships between the recording and telecommunication media are shown in Figure 5. The simplest communication medium is the messenger. The sender formulates and encodes a unit of information, then by speech, gesture, or other means conveys this message to a messenger who, carrying it in his head, covers the distance between sender and receiver, and delivers it orally. The next method involves a recording medium in which the recording is under the sender's control. The recorded message becomes tangible software for the system; it is transported to the receiver, where it is played back and displayed. Audio and video tapes, films and filmstrips are examples of such media. The printed page is also a medium of this type, but it differs from the others in that the receiver requires no complex piece of playback equipment for display. Instead, the receiver uses a highly developed skill to decode the message, or a second person possessing this skill acts as a decoder.

The third method utilizes electronic transmission instead of transportation to carry the message from sender to receiver. Further, those media that have direct counterparts in both the telemedia and recording-media groups are capable of three additional methods which combine telecommunication and recording in various ways.

Now let us examine the communication model we have been discussing in somewhat greater detail. If the message is to be contained in a program, the sender will put it through a production process prior to transmission or recording. He may

*Thus, the word "tele," meaning "far" in the original Greek, has been frequently used in naming these media.

then elect to transmit it directly in real time, or to record it and transmit it later. For example, delayed transmission is the most widely used method in present-day television broadcasting; programs are recorded on video tape when convenient to the scheduling of the studios, and later transmitted when convenient to the program schedule. Control over the time of communication may also be exercised by the receiver at the other end of the process. Thus a school may pick up and record ITV programs at the time they are broadcast, playing them back later, often several times, to fit them better into existing school schedules. The various points in the process where time control is possible are shown by the blocks in Figure 5 marked "storage." At the receiving end, either playback or reception may take place at the point of display (as when a tape is played back in the classroom, or a television receiver is tuned in), or they may take place at a central point such as a local school and then be piped to the intended audience via a local transmission system. The extra line from local playback, joining the transmission route, indicates the possibility of playback over a local transmission system, rather than at the point of display.


## LIVE VERSUS RECORDED BROADCASTING

Both radio and television broadcasting began as nearly exclusively live media, adding the element of central recording (see Figure 5) only when recording systems had been developed with sufficient high-fidelity that it was not possible for the general audience to distinguish between recorded and live presentation.

There has been considerable difference of opinion since the first days of the broadcast media concerning the merits or advantages of live telecommunication versus the playback of recordings. Most broadcasters have agreed, for example, that the "newsness" of news broadcasts and the "actuality" of special events and sports contests requires the immediacy of live transmission. "This is Ed Murrow in London" carried a significance for real-time broadcasting which it could never have for a recording.

There was even a strong case made, in the days of live television drama, to support the stand that a live television drama was an actual performance, like the living theater, and therefore required the actuality of the live broadcast. Live television drama, it was maintained, conveyed a feeling of audience participation never possible when a film was transmitted. This effect may have been more apparent than real; actually, measurement of overt audience response had never really been possible. The discussions did not die, however, even after the near disappearance of live drama on television.

Similar arguments are also heard pro and con on the question of live-production versus recording media in relation to instruction. Surely live presentation is required if the instructor is to receive questions via a feedback system and adapt to them in the course of his presentation. It is even considered essential for some administrative uses, such as announcements of school events and the regular visits of the school superintendent with his staff. The institutions that use live television for lesson presentation, however, justify it on the basis of lack of video tape recording (VTR) equipment, lack of funds for the tape inventory required for all recorded presentations, and the advantage of possible revision and improvement when lessons are produced afresh each time they are presented. There is also another viable argument for live transmission: The studio teacher who knows he is recording something for all posterity may be frozen into formality.

In general, however, the central recording of a lesson at a time that is convenient for production, and the playback of the lesson later, when it is convenient to the school schedule (that is, delayed transmission), has not been considered less effective than live transmission. There is great doubt that learners distinguish any difference among live transmission, delayed transmission and the transmission of recordings. There is little evidence, however, to determine just what learners do imagine a given medium to be, and what difference it would make, if any, if they learned that something was really recorded when they thought it was live, or really live when they thought it was recorded.

It seems likely that the learner will tend to respond to a program either as if it were the most commonly experienced mode, or as if it were the more desirable of the two possibilities. In general, since seeing something that is happening at a distance is somewhat more magical than seeing something that happened in the past, school children, at least, would probably react to video tape as though it were a live broadcast. This will probably change as portable video tape machines become increasingly familiar in the classroom and video tape becomes the more common consciously experienced medium.

## MESSAGES, PROGRAMS AND MEDIA

The possibility of incorporating the message into a program, we have said, is the condition which distinguishes the communication system from the transmitting or the recording system. The message, incidentally, is not the medium, any more than the medium is the message. There is nothing to be gained in this discussion by going along with McLuhan's semantic trickery and using message to mean the general social importance or significance of the medium. We shall use message as everyone else does, to mean the information which is communicated, and medium to mean the means whereby communication is accomplished.

The message or content is generally organized into a form called the *program*. "Program" is a very broad term and has many meanings, at least two of which are applicable here: (1) a unified presentation occupying a discrete period of time and having a beginning, a middle, and an end (e.g., a television program), or (2) an organized activity, such as programmed instruction. A program in this sense is unified and discrete, as in definition 1, but it is also designed according to specifications related to its output objectives. An instructional program, thus, would be based on clearly defined behavioral objectives, would present instruction in small increments, would constantly elicit and evaluate learner response, and would provide knowledge of results. Any communication medium is capable of this degree of programming, even though it does not have a feedback system associated with it.

Programs are rarely involved in the communication of simple information to the *information user*. The message is merely encoded in words or pictures, then further encoded in the technical transmission or recording code of the medium.

In instructional communication, the content of the medium consists of both the message and the program containing it. The message is *what* the instructor says, and the program is *how* he says it.* A curriculum of specific information and general concepts as presented in a book would differ from the same curriculum as presented in a film, for example. Each medium requires the message to be encoded into a different format, using a different set of techniques, and resulting in a different kind of program. *"The medium shapes the message."*** Within each medium, however, there is a wide variation in the kinds of programs that can be devised. There are many kinds of books, for example, illustrating the many ways of laying out type and illustrations.

The model shown in Figure 6 summarizes the points that have just been made. There are nine successive stages in the encoding and decoding of a message for communication via an instructional medium. Stage 1 is the conception of the message. A certain amount of information is generated out of the instructor's knowledge, some of which may have also been retrieved from his access to information storage systems (see Figure 1). Stage 2 is the first encoding. The information is expressed in language, which need not necessarily be verbal—it may be the language of pictures, for example, or of gestures, or combinations of these. There may even be a subsystem called script-writing which allows the

*"Says" is used here in the general sense of expressing or presenting.

**Personal communication from C. R. Carpenter, Pennsylvania State University, July 1969.

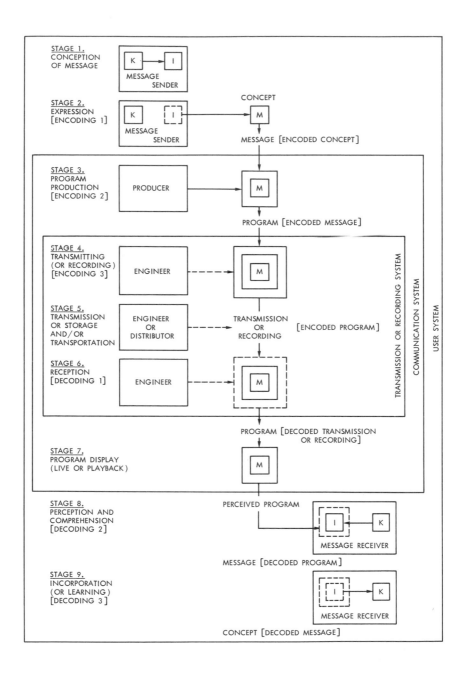

*Figure 6.* Stages in communication via a communication medium.

message, plus the program which will carry the message, to be temporarily expressed in written words.

Stage 3, where the message is further encoded into a program, may occur at the same time as message expression, or it may occur later. In Stage 4 the third and final encoding takes place when the program is transferred by technical means into the analog or digital code of the recording or transmitting medium.

Stage 5 is the actual transmission of the program (if a telecommunication medium is being used) or the combination of storage and transportation of the program, if it is a recording medium.

Stage 6 is the first stage of decoding, where the program is transferred into a perceptible form. In Stage 7 the message receiver—in this case, the learner—views the program (reads the book, listens to the tape, etc.). He selectively decodes and comprehends the message, applying his knowledge of the code—if he understands the language in which it is encoded and if the message has relevance to him (Stage 8). The last stage, Stage 9, which does not always take place, is in the case of an instructional user system, learning. This the learner must do for himself; however, the instructor (message sender) generally designs the message and its program to facilitate this process as much as possible. In telecommunication all these stages *may* take place simultaneously, or nearly so, as one program segment follows another through the course of the program. In live television, for instance, at least stages 4 through 8 are generally simultaneous. Stage 9 may take a little thought and review.

If, as is frequently the case, a program is communicated via a combination of media—recorded on video tape, for example, and subsequently broadcast or transmitted by wire—another step must be added to the total process. In Stage 4 the program is encoded into the magnetic analog code of the recording medium (video tape) as shown, but before it can be transmitted it must be transferred to the electrical analog code of television. This is not a further encoding; it is a transfer process in which the program is simultaneously decoded from its magnetic form and encoded into

electrical impulses. The next decoding takes place nearly simultaneously at the other end of the transmission path, in which case
the program may be either decoded immediately and viewed (as
shown in Figure 5) or transferred again to video tape to be
decoded and viewed at a later time.

Certain media, such as microform and teletype, rarely carry
programs, since they are generally used only for the simple
transmission of information. In these cases the program encoding
and decoding stages (Stages 3 and 7 of the process) do not exist,
and the entire process consists of only seven steps.

These primarily information media are: picturephone, telephone, facsimile and teletype among the telecommunication
media, and microform, video file, and punched paper tape among
the recording media. If the reader would prefer to think of these
as information media rather than communication media, and
remove them from the list on Table 1, he will have some
justification for doing so. When simple information is to be
conveyed, a full communication medium is not required; merely a
recording or a transmitting system will suffice. However, there are
program uses of such media. There is at least one instance of
microfiche being used in a teaching machine, where a succession of
images are very definitely organized into a program. Video signals,
filed on magnetic tape or disc, either as still or motion images, are
also being used as a source of instructional materials in a growing
number of random-access and dial-access systems.

Thus, in classifying communication systems, we must be
careful to consider more than current uses; a lasting classification
must be based on capabilities and potentials rather than present
applications.

In the planning of communication systems, the hardware-
software dichotomy is an important consideration; too often in
the past, promising devices have proved unsuccessful in use
because of the lack of a sufficient and continuing supply of
program software. It should be pointed out here that the software
availability problem is peculiar to the program media, and is not
applicable to telemedia which are being used simply for informa-

tion transmission. Libraries of stored microforms, video files, and such software are of course as important to information storage systems as program materials are to instructional media.


## COMMUNICATION MEDIA Versus COMMUNICATION AIDS

The use of a communication medium in instruction makes it unnecessary for an instructor to actually be present when and where his instructional presentation is received. This separation is possible because the instructional program contains all necessary parts of the message: audio and/or visual stimuli, and exposition of some kind to give them the requisite significance. The exposition is nearly always verbal—either spoken or written. The medium carrying this complete message is being used as a communication medium. Considerable confusion in thinking has resulted from the practice of applying the general term *media* to both complete communication media such as films and video tapes, and to *aids* such as charts and slides that a lecturer might use to illustrate his remarks. These instructional aids do not carry the entire instructional load but serve only to support a classroom teacher's face-to-face presentation. Both communication aids and communication media have traditionally been classed as "audio-visual media," and in education as "instructional media." Whatever meaning we accept for the general term "media," it is important that we make a clean distinction between media which are only communication *aids* and media which are complete communications *systems*.

As a general rule, the communication medium contains verbal exposition, whereas the communication aid does not. A device that does not contain narration, commentary, dialogue, or captions in its software, such as a slide or overhead transparency projector, is generally useful only as an aid to instruction; verbal exposition by a live classroom teacher must accompany its presentation. On the other hand, if the device does contain its own exposition, it cannot readily be used as an instructional aid; the sound must be turned off or the printed captions edited out, if the words of the program are not to interfere with what the classroom teacher is trying to say. Thus, for most purposes the two categories, communication aid and communication medium, are mutually exclusive.

Three situations should be noted which may look like exceptions, but which actually do not affect the rule: (1) A self-contained film, a recorded speech, or a piece of music may be presented not as instruction but as a subject for study in and of itself. This would constitute neither an instructional aid nor an instructional medium. (2) A short segment of sound film, a filmstrip, or another instructional device may be integrated into a classroom lesson presentation. This is a clear case of the use of a communication medium, however brief the use may be. When a film is on the screen, for example, the teacher will, in effect, turn the students over to the medium and expect them to give it their full attention. The teacher may assist or supplement it by occasional comments or provocative questions, but the medium is doing the teaching. (3) A classroom teacher may interpose comments during the running of a film, relate it to the recent experience of the class, name individuals to respond to questions put by the film, etc. In this case the teacher is assisting the film, not the other way around.

The main reason for this insistence upon a clear distinction between instructional aids and communication media is the decided difference between them in their importance to education. The difference is far more significant than a distinction between incompleteness and completeness. The instructional *aid* generally plays a minor role in a limited-output system, in which an instructor making a lesson presentation reaches no more learners than his classroom can hold. Except for becoming more widely and effectively used, instructional aids in the classroom will probably never play a more important role than they do today. Certainly they are not likely to change the nature of instruction.

Communication media, on the other hand, can be put at the core of a system, the output of which could be staggering.

Recording media and telemedia, able to reach tremendous numbers of learners with a single lesson presentation, are capable of both raising the overall quality of instruction and greatly extending its reach. Even the instructional aids will play a more significant role when they are part of the programming of communication media. The communication media have the potential to transform instruction as much as they have transformed society through the transmission of mass entertainment and information over the last fifty years.

One trend should be mentioned in regard to this impending revolution in learning: the trend toward independent learning and self-instruction. Communication media may play their most important instructional role in this area. Because no educational system will be capable of imparting to an individual all the knowledge he will need in the future, learners will be increasingly trained in the skills of information retrieval and self-instruction. Individual study carrels, autoinstructional devices, single-concept films, and individual cartridge projectors are examples of technological developments within this trend. Note, however, it is the communication media with their built-in verbal exposition which will be used in self-instruction, not instructional aids. The instructional aids, limited to functioning as illustrative material for face-to-face teacher presentation, not self-contained and not self-explanatory, will only enter into self-instruction as they are incorporated into communication media programs.

## REPRODUCIBILITY, AN IMPORTANT CHARACTERISTIC OF COMMUNICATION MEDIA

One of the reasons for the importance of communication media in our rapidly developing society is the fact that senders of messages find it increasingly difficult to deliver them in person. Face-to-face communication is still generally felt to be the most effective technique—in the performing arts, in persuasion, and in instruction (except for lectures in large halls, where the communication is face-to-*distant*-face). However, our societies have grown far too large for personal contact between all those who have something to say and those who might want to hear (or see) it. But in making it possible for one person to communicate with another at a distance, and/or at another time, the inventors of the communication media have opened up a vast new dimension. The dimension is measured by the number of people that a single message may reach, and the key characteristic that makes this dimension possible is reproducibility.

Telecommunication media can transmit a single message to countless widely separated viewer/listeners at one time. Recording media can put a single message into permanent form which can be multiplied into many identical copies and delivered countless times for countless reader/viewer/listeners over a long period of time. This is not only convenient but extremely economical; witness the huge success of books.

The reproducibility of communicated messages via the media is one of the major achievements of technological civilization. "Margaret Mead has reported that when she brought several copies of the same book to a Pacific island there was great excitement. The natives had seen books, but only one copy of each, which they had assumed to be unique. Their astonishment at the identical character of several books was a natural response to what is after all the most magical and potent aspect of print and mass production. It involves a principle of extension by homogenization that is the key to understanding Western power."[2]

There are four kinds of reproducibility, three of which can make possible large economies of scale in communication:

1.  Point-to-point transmission (one reproduction in one distant place).
2.  Point-to-many-point transmission (simultaneous reproductions in many distant places).
3.  Recording (many sequential reproductions of a single recording at different times and places).
4.  Printing (many duplications made of one recording,

thereby increasing the possible number of sequential reproductions at different times and places).

The first kind of reproducibility is based on simple transmission. The telephone speaker's voice, for example, is reproduced in the listener's ear. If the transmission takes place within normal earshot or other perceptual range, such as within a room, it can be called amplification or magnification. For telecommunication to exist, the sender and receiver must be separated by distance greater than normal sight or hearing range. This kind of reproducibility is on a one-to-one basis—the message is reproduced once in one place. Telecommunication media, when used in the individual mode, have only this level of reproducibility.

The mass telecommunication media, such as live radio and television, add another dimension of reproducibility. Via these media, a message is simultaneously reproduced for listeners or viewers in many different physical locations. The reception of the message is multiplied by the medium.

The recording media exhibit still other kinds of reproducibility. Once a message is recorded it can be stored, carried from place to place, and reproduced sequentially many times in many places, over a long period of time. This kind of reproducibility may be further extended by duplicating the software containing the message. Films and books, for example, are *printed*; certain other media are said to be *dubbed* or *duplicated.* The message itself is multiplied by this use of the recording medium.

When recorded messages are transmitted by telecommunication media, they may have the simultaneous reproducibility of telecommunication while retaining the sequential reproducibility of the recording media. That is to say, a film or video tape may, if broadcast, be received simultaneously over a wide geographical area and, in addition, via multiple copies, may eventually reach a much larger number of viewer/listeners over a period of time. While telemedia released communication from the constraints of place, recording media released it from the constraints of both place and time.

## THE EVALUATION OF COMMUNICATION

We have already noted that the purpose of a communication system is to accept a message, build it into a program, transmit or record it, and display it finally before its intended audience or audiences. The communication medium, as a system, is not involved in the choice of message content, nor in the uses and purposes of the message once it has been conveyed. *People* who work in communication media may be concerned with these things, but only as they consider or take part in functions which are part of the *user* system.

It is only within the context of the user system that a communication system can be evaluated. No value judgment as to the success or failure, the efficiency, feasibility, or effectiveness of either a communication system or an individual communication can be made from a point of view which is strictly within the system itself. The purpose of communication is inherent in the user system; the communication medium, in one way or another, helps the user system to function. Sometimes this purpose may be the same as the purpose of the user system itself, as in the case of public relations films within a public relations system. In other cases, communication media may serve relatively minor functions of the user system, and must be coordinated by the user with many other functions (which may or may not include communication media) before the user system itself can be successful in achieving *its* purposes. Classroom instruction is a case to illustrate this point.

A common first reaction to the proposed application of a communication medium is that it must surely be less effective than face-to-face communication with an individual or group. If effective is understood to mean "achieving the desired results," this can often be true; however, there are several factors which can tend to make the reverse true. When these factors are understood and emphasized, many kinds of communication can be considerably more effectively presented via a medium than face-to-face. To exemplify this point, let us consider a specific communication medium, television, in respect to a specific user system, instruction.

When television is introduced into an instructional system to replace certain traditional elements of that system, it can have *qualitative* advantages over what has been done before. Television lessons can be better prepared and can bring better teachers into the average classroom, despite the tendency of media presentations to be impersonal. To some people, this impersonality seems like a large obstacle to effectiveness. Also, the large-scale or mass aspects of the media bring to mind an unfortunate analogy with mass production and assembly-line manufacture. It is often expected, therefore, that students who receive lesson presentation by instructional media will achieve poorer results than students who have been taught by traditional classroom methods. If this is so, it has not been detected in a very large number of comparative studies.[3] Neither has any evidence been found to show that presentation via an instructional medium, *per se,* results in any *greater* scholastic achievement than classroom presentation. A recent study reviewed some 421 comparisons of instructional television (ITV) with traditional teaching, of which 308, or 73 percent, showed no significant difference in achievement between experimental and control groups. In 15 percent there was a significant difference favoring television, and in only 12 percent was there a significant difference favoring the traditional classroom methods.[4]

These results have, of course, been interpreted in many ways, depending on the prior bias of the interpreter. Opponents of instructional television, for example, see in such data no indication of any advantage to using the medium, as far as achievement is concerned. Proponents say that ITV has been shown to be at least as effective as conventional methods, so it may be used where economies are indicated, without fear of lowering standards. Some skeptics say the failure to show any significant difference may be due to the inadequacy of measuring methods, and others suggest that it is due to the paucity of our knowledge about the learning process—in their view, both ITV and conventional methods may be equally inept.

It should be noted that many of these studies have failed to measure some of the most important factors. In order to be scientifically valid, most were designed to rigidly control all variables, except the one being examined—television versus face-to-face instruction. In real life, however, the introduction of a new significant element into a system generally affects all other elements of the system, and in these secondary, usually unmeasured effects, instructional media can often provide advantages. We will examine several indirect effects which may result from a typical use of television in instruction—basic presentation—the initial exposition of a given subject matter. There are ways in which ITV lessons can be superior by usual standards to classroom lessons and, by these same standards, can be more effective in producing learning.* The same effects can also be obtained through the use of various other communication media in instruction.

*1. ITV lessons can provide audiovisual enrichment.* Audio and visual materials of many kinds may be used in television production. Often these are the same kinds of materials that are used as instructional aids in the classroom. However, the television teacher can spend much more time than the classroom teacher on the selection and/or production of such materials, and generally has the assistance of librarians and craftsmen, as well as a wider range of materials from which to select. Thus the televised lesson can be greatly enhanced in audiovisual complexity, compared with the average classroom presentation with generally available instruction aids. Insofar as this is constructive rather than distracting, it can lead to increased effectiveness.

*2. More effort can be put into the preparation of ITV lessons.* Since television lessons reach many learners in many classrooms, more time and energy can go into them than is available, in the economics of school instruction, for the lesson

---

*Chu and Schramm found their 421 comparisons, for all their inadequacies, gave TV a net advantage over face-to-face instruction of 10 percent at the elementary level, 7 percent at the secondary, and 15 percent at the adult level. At the college level, face-to-face instruction showed a slight net advantage of 3 percent.

which is to be given only once to one group of learners. Assuming that this energy is well directed, the ITV lesson can be better thought out, better organized, and better presented than the usual classroom lesson.

*3. ITV lessons can raise the average level of lesson quality in a school system.* When television is used in basic presentation, it replaces a large number of good, bad and mediocre classroom presentations of the same material, with a single televised presentation of, presumably, the highest available quality. The medium thus offers the opportunity to raise the *average* level of effectiveness of presentation of the given lesson material throughout the system. This in turn can help assure a higher overall level of student achievement.

*4. ITV lesson presentation is public, not private.* The television lesson is presented in a more public context than the classroom lesson, because it is transmitted (even though this may be within a closed-circuit system); administrators, colleagues, visitors, etc., are likely to see it, since it is not confined to the relative privacy of the single classroom. This makes it more ego-involving for the performer and participants and motivates greater care and effort in its preparation. It should be noted, however, that if this factor creates nervousness or camera fright, it will often cause the kind of stiffness and formality that is destructive to communication. Under these conditions, it frequently happens that a teacher who is very effective in the classroom is deadly on ITV. With proper direction this handicap can be readily overcome, however.

*5. ITV lessons can release the classroom teacher for other important functions.* Perhaps the most important contribution of the media to the improvement of instruction is an indirect one. Communication media, especially when programmed, can fulfill many instructional functions traditionally performed by the classroom teacher. Lesson presentation, drill and practice, and review may be done as well via a medium as by a classroom teacher. On the other hand, probably the most important things that happen in a classroom are things that only the teacher can provide: interaction, understanding, encouragement and informal progress appraisal. The teacher, as group leader, can greatly help the learner to relate well with his peers and to learn how to become part of a social unit. At the elementary level, only a teacher can constitute an adult model to emulate; only a teacher can take a sincere personal interest in a child. There is little enough of these priceless ingredients in any classroom. Where the use of a medium can release teacher energies for these essential functions, the entire instructional system cannot fail to benefit.

It should be noted that all five of these points are concerned with how the medium is used; none are inherent within the medium itself. The first says that the user can present more and better stimuli, if he wishes; the second says that he may feasibly put in more preparation effort, if he wishes; the third says that this may be used to raise the average level of lesson quality, if the user wishes to spread it widely enough; the fifth says that the user may take advantage of the opportunity to redeploy teacher energies, if he wishes. Only the fourth, the public nature of lesson presentation, may appear to be inherent in the medium itself, because of the feature of reproducibility. Even this factor, however, is dependent on utilization; many ITV lesson presentations are displayed in only two or three classrooms, used only in a single course, or are purposely not recorded and reused (at the wish of the TV instructors involved).

Because the research has concentrated so much on discovering instructional advantages inherent in the medium itself, the effects of these possible resultant changes to *other* elements of the instructional system have been largely neglected.

If instruction is to be improved by better communication, the improvement must come from *what* is communicated, not from *how* the message is conveyed. The design of an instructional message, plus the way in which the received message is integrated and coordinated into the other functions of the user system, will determine the degree of success of the user system far more than the mere choice of medium to be used. This is to say, *instructional* *method* is far more significant than instructional medium.* A good application of a communication medium in instruction is characterized by thorough integration of (1) program design and production, (2) medium of transmission or recording, and (3) display equipment configuration, into the instructional method in which it plays a role. Thus its effectiveness, its success or failure, is dependent on the success or failure of the instructional method which incorporates it.

Too often program materials in film, television, radio, and other communication media are evaluated according to criteria which are not relevant to the use to which they will be put. Often the criteria are derived from some entirely different user system for which the program was never intended and in which the purposes to be served are altogether different. The prime example of this is the instructional film evaluated by the standards of entertainment. This point is discussed in detail in the appendix to this volume.

## WHAT CAUSES FAILURE OF COMMUNICATION?

The causes for breakdown in communication are to be found within the technical transmission or recording subsystem, within the program display subsystem, the program production subsystem, and even more basically, outside the communication system itself, within the message origination function of the user system. These areas are listed in order of ascending importance as sources of communication failure, and will be discussed in that order.

*Chu and Schramm conclude that "...the research seems to suggest that effective use of television grows out of attention to the basic requirements of good teaching, rather than to any fanciness that might be peculiar to television."

## TRANSMISSION OR RECORDING FAILURE

Failure of transmission or recording is a technical matter, caused by equipment failure, or faulty human operation, resulting in (1) loss of either partial or total communication, or (2) impairment of communication due to the introduction of noise. It is almost a truism that the more complex a piece of hardware, the greater the probability of failure of some part (the shorter the "mean time between failures"). Complex computers, to give an extreme example, are generally "down" about a third of the time. To this must be added the increased probability of failure due to use of the least expensive parts and workmanship in products where low initial cost is a prime factor in sales. Still another factor is to be found in the rapid development and change in communication equipment, from one season to the next, serving a market primarily interested in "the newest," "the latest," rather than "the most reliable." This high rate of obsolescence precludes the perfection of a single model through gradual minor changes, as for example the Volkswagen car, and requires the constant testing out of new models and devices by the customer under conditions of regular use. It is no surprise that equipment reliability has been such a problem in the underdeveloped countries, where maintenance and repair facilities are meager, and that many of the more complex audiovisual systems are not feasible there. Broadcasting systems, especially those which depend on commercial income and to whom down-time means heavy financial loss, find it necessary to have duplicate equipment in use attitude ready for immediate replacement. Television film projectors, for instance, have dual lamp housings automated so that lamp failure results in immediate bulb replacement. Synchronizing pulse generators, a key item of equipment for television program origination, are regularly manufactured in pairs, with automated changeover in case of failure. Television remote pickups from ball parks, scenes of special events, and the like, are provided with standby microwave links, standby cameras, and standby audio transmission lines, as insurance against failure.

In the case of recording systems, recording, playback and program display equipment can cause similar technical problems. Distribution by transportation is analogous to transmission in the telecommunication medium. Here, loss or delay in the mails, in the messenger system, or on the part of a previous user of materials whose responsibility it is to send the program on to the next user (bicycling), is sometimes due to transportation equipment trouble, but most often to human factors and can be just as serious as transmission failure in telecommunication systems.

The procedure of "preventive maintenance" can reduce unexpected equipment failure, by replacing weak elements before they fail, but only at the cost of additional maintenance hours and added down-time.

Noise is a term which has come to mean any unwanted signal, whether sound or picture, which obscures or obliterates the communication. We are all familiar with radio static, television snow and interference, cross talk (unwanted programs superimposed in the background of the wanted), and various other sorts of electronic noise. Noise in films and slides can take the form of excess graininess of image, excess dirt or scratches on the film, and other results of laboratory failure such as excess contrast, making it difficult to distinguish details in the highlight or shadow areas. Sometimes noise is introduced by equipment malfunctioning, such as hum in audio systems, glitches and roll-overs in television switching; more often it enters from the outside, such as static in radio or dirt on film. The best preventative for noise seems to be constant care: careful shielding of equipment from outside radiation (broadcast signals, static, etc.), careful maintenance of equipment to prevent the occurrence of interior noise, care and cleanliness in every stage of a photographic operation, and care in the adjustment and operation of all equipment.

## PROGRAM DISPLAY SUBSYSTEM FAILURES

Looking now at the program display subsystem, we may note

additional sources of equipment failure, due to the same hardware and human factors listed above, aggravated by the fact that display equipment is usually the most cheaply built (to attract a large market) and is operated by people with a low level of technical competence. In the Washington County, Maryland, school system, which has some 750 television receivers operating in school classrooms, maintenance records for one of the early years of operation showed that 45 percent of the service calls to classrooms were resolved by plugging the receiver's power cord back into the wall, from whence the janitor, possibly, had dislodged it during his cleaning the night before.

Projection display of audiovisual materials is traditionally plagued by display failures, most of which are due to human factors such as lack of preplanning or failure to safeguard adequately against accident. To many of us it may seem that someone will trip over a cord and disconnect a projector at least once every time a film or slide projector is operated in the same room with an audience. At one national convention of an audiovisual association (of all places) the incidence of display failure was close to 100 percent. Screens were set up in meeting rooms opposite high windows which could not be curtained. Speakers arrived at the scheduled time of their speeches with sets of slides, films, etc., to find no projectors provided, or projectors of the wrong standard. When the right projector was on hand it failed to operate. One outside speaker converted his speech into a searing criticism of this condition. The following year a special A-V coordinator was assigned to each meeting to preplan, double-check, and take responsibility; the incidence of trouble dropped to an all-time low.

## PROGRAM PRODUCTION FAILURES

Even though all equipment and operators function flawlessly throughout the communication system, communication can still fail for human reasons, as we have just seen. Some of these failures can originate in the planning and production of the programs themselves. For example, program production itself can introduce noise.

We have already noted the tendency of many instructional film or TV producers to introduce elements of showmanship into their productions which sometimes impair these programs' effectiveness in achieving their primary purpose. These elements may be intended as attention-getting and attention-holding devices, but they are often referred to as "sugar coating on the pill" or "gimmicks and dancing girls." In one film intended for engineers, it was decided to have a series of verbally discussed items also displayed in print for additional clarity and emphasis. The film producer had these items printed on successively smaller cards. The entire set was held by a bathing-suited model as she stood facing the camera, at first covering her from neck to knee, then gradually revealing more of her lovely anatomy as she removed one card after another. Attention-getting and attention-holding? Without doubt. Clarifying and emphasizing of the ideas involved? Hardly. The introduction of distractions, when they divide or capture the attention of the viewer, can be as serious as noise which actually obscures the message.

At the other end of the pendulum swing, the producer may set his program in a style which is unpleasant to the viewer, such as a stiff and formal lecture, and achieve an emotional rejection by the viewer, who effectively turns the program off. At such moments of boredom the viewer's mind wanders, looking for distractions, fastening even upon idiosyncrasies in the speaker's manner for a fix of attention.

The producer may fail simply because he has constructed a poorly organized or structured program. If the presentation does not develop logically, it may be difficult to follow, and points may be lost because prerequisite ideas were not given first. This kind of failure is more commonly a fault of message design, to be discussed later.

A common fault is in the combining of visual materials with spoken words. Used properly, visuals may enhance words, and words may define and clarify visuals. Used badly, these two channels of information can fight one another, destroying both the perception of the visual and the understanding of the verbal.

The pace of the program can be another element where the wrong judgment can be made. If the program is paced too fast, and the ideas crowd upon the viewer faster than he can assimilate them (or even write them down in his notebook for later assimilation), they will be lost. If the program is paced too slow, so that ideas do not come fast enough to hold the viewer's interest and attention, he may turn off and not be reached at all.

## MESSAGE ORIGINATION FAILURES

We have discussed communication faults originating within the communication system itself, first the purely technical matters of hardware operation, and next, judgments of the planner and producer of the program software. The most serious matters, however, are not to be found in the communication system at all, but are involved in the conception of the message before it ever enters the communication medium. These failures involve the original encoding of the message, and exist when the message sender is not sufficiently familiar with those who are intended to receive the message, either concerning their general state of knowledge and attitude, or concerning their specific state of mental set under the specific conditions of the reception situation. A film used in a theater or auditorium, for example, where the mental set is for entertainment, cannot convey a serious instructional message as well as the same film in individual study use. It is a matter of choice of message.

Possibly the most common cause of ineffective communication is failure to encode the message in the receiver's language. Unfamiliar words, pictures of unfamiliar subjects, the enactment of unfamiliar actions, may not be comprehended. UNESCO recently made a detailed study of a large number of the best instructional films in the United States, with a view to adapting them for use in Latin America. The considered verdict was that even if the sound tracks were rewritten as well as translated, the unfamiliarity not only of cultural elements, but of flora and fauna as well, left *none* of them directly adaptable for Latin American use.*

Failure of comprehension is only one result of faulty encoding. Another is *mis*comprehension, called misunderstanding. Since almost all messages, audio or visual, depend on the understanding of words for their comprehension, it is essential that the words chosen by a message sender have the same meanings for the message receivers as he intends them to have. This is another area in which the message sender needs a thorough knowledge of his target audience.**

Pictures, we have found, can be highly ambiguous and need to be carefully explained, in words again, if they are not to create information misunderstandings. While it is said that the camera cannot lie, caption writers readily can, and the ends of political propaganda have often been served by giving an artificial meaning to an ambiguous photograph. Atrocity pictures from other wars are sometimes used to illustrate recent happenings. Still photographs capture only an instant in time: a snapshot at the moment of what may have been the single stamp of a foot on a cold morning can be identified as part of a gleeful dance of victory.

The objectives of persuasion and instruction systems require that messages must not only be perceived and comprehended, they must also be used and integrated by the receiver so as to change his outlook on life in some small manner, and alter his behavioral responses to various stimuli. It is intended that he undergo some change in attitude, skill, or knowledge. If this does not immediately take place, the instructional or persuasive communication

*Personal communication with Dr. Jose Garza y de Gerate, Instituto Latinoamericana de Cinematographia Educativa, Dom: Auditorio Nacional Ciudad de Mexico, Mexico, D.F.

**The field of general semantics has contributed much useful thinking in this area, with which any serious message sender should make himself familiar.

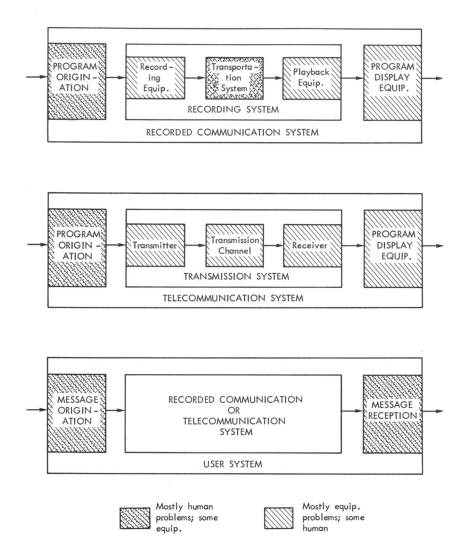

*Figure 7.* Sources of human and equipment problems.

need not be considered a complete failure. As we have said, communication via a medium is generally only a part of a larger combination of influences, many of which fall outside the communication system, but which must all contribute their small effects before a change becomes apparent and it can be said that persuasion or learning has taken place.

If a message is to be accepted by the receiver, and integrated into his knowledge or outlook on life, it must not only be perceived and comprehended, but it must strike him as pertinent and relevant to his needs and seem immediately useful. Thus, the tremendous importance of motivation in the teaching-learning process. Dr. E. W. Bollinger, in teaching instructional methods, used to say that he would prefer to spend 40 minutes of a class period motivating his students to want what he would give them in the final 10 minutes, than to spend the full 50 minutes presenting information in which they had no interest. Instructive or persuasive messages will probably fail unless they are accompanied or preceded by other persuasive messages (motivation) designed to alter the receiver's attitude toward the messages which will follow. Otherwise, such messages will constitute no more than interesting information, much like the extensive data on dates and heights of monuments which tourist guides dish out, to be noted, ummed or ahhed about, and quickly forgotten.

The message sender needs to be sure that the reactions and responses he wants are actually evoked in the receiver, and that any change in behavior that he expects to take place actually does occur. For this reason he needs to monitor his receivers, or samples of his receiver population, and to establish some sort of feedback communication system to let him know whether his messages are succeeding in their purpose. The trend is toward the pretesting of messages (and the program in which they are contained) on representative sample audiences. The difficulty of this approach, however, is that most of the measurable changes in the message receiver do not occur directly as a result of any one or series of communications, but as the cumulative result, as mentioned above, of all of the coordinated elements within the user system. It has long been recognized that a learner does not learn from lectures or television presentations alone, but as a combined result of such factors as: prior motivation and preparation, plus later thought and discussion; review and response practice; reinforcement for correct responses; and frequent opportunities to apply his knowledge in situations of actual use.

This discussion is somewhat summarized in Figure 7, where the two types of communication systems are again diagrammed, plus a generalized user system. Shading indicates those areas where human problems are predominant, and those where equipment is usually the main source of communication failure.

# 4.

# A Proposed Taxonomy of Communication Media

What are these media that are becoming so important in our expanding world, and what can we do with them? The first step in answering these questions is to classify the media so that some generalizations can be made about them. Since communication media are all the product of man's inventiveness, there is no natural relationship among them to discover; we must choose some artificial means of classification. The best means, we may assume, will be the means that is the most useful. Prior to this, however, we must establish a set of criteria with which we can distinguish between (a) a medium and nonmedium, (b) one medium and another, and (c) a single medium and a multimedia application.

## COMMUNICATION-MEDIA CRITERIA

The first criterion for distinguishing a communication medium from a nonmedium is that it be *capable of communicating messages that are complete within themselves* and do not require face-to-face verbal narration at the point of reception. This criterion distinguishes the communication media from communication aids.

The second criterion is that *the system be capable of reproducing a program* either by simultaneous reproducibility (point-to-point, or point-to-many-point) or sequential reproducibility (recording or recording and printing). The capability of reproduction may not be exercised in every application; it is possible in any recording medium, for instance, that program production may result in a single copy for a single use. The fact that the system is *capable* of reproducibility, however, qualifies it under this criterion. These first two criteria, then, distinguish a communication medium from a nonmedium.

The next two criteria are useful in distinguishing one medium from another. They have been used in deciding which systems are separate media and which are varieties or subclasses of other media. Criterion 3 states that *a system is a separate medium if it utilizes a different combination of the five ways of representing information\* from the combination used by its near relatives.* Thus the sound motion picture is considered to be a separate medium from the silent film, even though the equipment configurations are so similar that many hardware items are interchangeable between the two. Through the addition of audio, the nature of the medium was substantially changed, requiring quite different production techniques and opening up a broad new range of uses.

Criterion 4 states that *a medium is distinct if it is based on devices (hardware) that are of a different kind from those of its near relatives*—that is, different combinations of electrical, mechanical, photographic and/or optical processes. Thus audio-disc recording (a mechanical record) has been classed as a separate medium from audio-tape recording (a magnetic record), even though the same program could be recorded on either and the listener who heard only the result might not know or care about the difference. Application of this criterion is somewhat arbitrary,

---

\*Sound, picture, line graphics, print, motion.

however, as demonstrated by the fact that FM and AM radio are not separated. The difference between these, while great enough that messages transmitted by one system cannot be received by the other, is still not sufficient to be considered a difference in kind.

Criterion 5 distinguishes single communication media from multimedia combinations. Criterion 5 thus states that in a communication medium all program elements are transmitted via the same system or distributed together. Sometimes a program display is combined with additional displays that require their own hardware systems (radio broadcast combined with projected slides, for instance). When the additional elements are not encoded into the primary medium and/or constitute materials that did not come from sender to receiver along with the primary message in a single "package," the whole may be called an instructional communication system, but not a single medium.

It is not uncommon, for example, for an audio tape to be planned for use along with a student workbook, with the intent that illustrations in the book are to be viewed while the tape is heard. (The workbook also may provide a medium for overt learner responses.) This is an instructional system which integrates two communication media simultaneously: audio tape and printed page. The two cannot be called a single medium even though they are integrated into a single instructional system.

At least three of the telemedia possess augmented forms in which locally displayed elements are coordinated with the transmitted elements. These are telelecture, radiovision and telewritevision. Radiovision is often discussed as a separate medium, whereas telelecture and telewritevision are generally considered to be simply augmented forms of telephone and telewriting. For our purposes, all three of these systems will be considered to be simultaneous multimedia systems in which an audio telemedium is augmented by the simultaneous display of recorded visual elements.

There are cases that are difficult to distinguish. For example, the sound filmstrip with separate sound might be said to consist of an audio-disc (or audio-tape) system in coordination with a silent-filmstrip system. Because both of these systems are integrated into a single piece of display hardware, however, and because both filmstrip and record are included in the same package, separate-sound filmstrip qualifies as a discrete medium.

The ultimate judgment of classification will probably be based on usage as much as logic. If an audio and printed-materials system became widely popular, such as the currently used audio tape and workbook system for language teaching, both materials would probably be distributed in the same package, and they would come to be described by a single name as a single system. Thus we can foresee the possibility of successful combinations of means, which are considered multimedia applications today, becoming integrated in hardware and packaging and becoming single and discrete new media tomorrow.

In summary, let us briefly review the criteria which a system must meet if it is to be called a communication medium:

1.  The system must be capable of conveying a complete message; it must be self-contained and self-supporting.
2.  The system must be capable of reproducing the message in the same or another form in one or more of the following ways: simultaneously in a distant place; simultaneously in many distant places; sequentially over a period of time; sequentially and simultaneously in many times and places.
3.  The system must involve a unique combination of the five ways of representing information.
4.  The system must use a special equipment system (for one or all of the various encoding, transmitting, and decoding functions).
5.  A single medium includes only the program elements that reach the receiver through one transmission and/or recording and distribution system.

Criteria 1 and 2 distinguish communication media and aids; criteria 3 and 4 distinguish one communication medium from another; and criterion 5 distinguishes discrete communication media from multimedia applications.

The communication media of which the author is aware are listed by class in Table 1. Each of these media, of course, has its varieties (for example, the various gauges of film). There may be other clearly defined media which have been inadvertently omitted from the list; almost certainly, others will evolve in the future.

There are points of correlation between the telecommunication and recording media. In Table 1, media which have counterparts are placed on the same line. Several telecommunication media appear to have recording-media counterparts, which could possibly be used to record messages in advance for later transmission via these media. There is a basic difference between a telemedium and its recording-medium counterpart; they have quite different characteristics and uses and should not be confused.*

## CLASSES OF MEDIA

In the past, communication media have been classified in various ways. Purpose, for example, used as a basis for classification, divides the field into such classes as information, instruction and entertainment. This is really a classification of user systems though, not of the media themselves. Mass media, those media which have so pervaded our society that they are used by very large numbers of people, may be distinguished from media which are limited to group or individual use. Media have also been

*A somewhat different view is taken by Winslow. (Winslow, K. *Educational/ Instructional Broadcasting,* September/October, 1968.) He makes no basic distinction between television and video tape, seeing video tape as a device for storage/retrieval of television—a means of communication delay. Television, in his view, is an audio-motion-visual medium in real-time; video tape, the same thing in delayed-time. While this concept serves the case of video recording, and probably applies as well to recorded still-television, recorded telewriting, and punched paper tape, it cannot be generalized to other media.

| TELECOMMUNICATION | Sound | Picture | Line Graphic | Print | Motion | RECORDING |
|---|---|---|---|---|---|---|
| CLASS I: AUDIO-MOTION-VISUAL MEDIA | | | | | | |
|  | X | X | X | X | X | Sound film |
| Television | X | X | X | X | X | { Video tape / Film TV recording |
|  | X | X | X | X | X | Holographic recording |
| Picturephone | X | X | X | X | X |  |
| CLASS II: AUDIO-STILL-VISUAL MEDIA | | | | | | |
| Slow-scan TV / Time-shared TV } | X | X | X | X |  | Recorded still TV |
|  | X | X | X | X |  | Sound filmstrip |
|  | X | X | X | X |  | Sound slide-set |
|  | X | X | X | X |  | Sound-on-slide |
|  | X | X | X | X |  | Sound page |
|  | X | X | X | X |  | Talking book |
| CLASS III: AUDIO-SEMIMOTION MEDIA | | | | | | |
| Telewriting | X |  | X | X | x | Recorded telewriting |
| CLASS IV: MOTION-VISUAL MEDIA | | | | | | |
|  |  | X | X | X | X | Silent film |
| CLASS V: STILL-VISUAL MEDIA | | | | | | |
| Facsimile |  | X | X | X |  | Printed page |
|  |  | X | X | X |  | Filmstrip |
|  |  | X | X | X |  | Picture set |
|  |  | X | X | X |  | Microform |
|  |  | X | X | X |  | Video file |
| CLASS VI: AUDIO MEDIA | | | | | | |
| Telephone } / Radio } | X |  |  |  |  | { Audio disc / Audio tape |
| CLASS VII: PRINT MEDIA | | | | | | |
| Teletype |  |  |  | X |  | Punched paper tape |

## The Communication Media

*Table 1*

divided into those that are essentially two-way and are used for intercommunication purposes, like the telephone, and those that are essentially one-way. McLuhan speaks about "hot" and "cool" media.[5] A more valuable approach than this is to divide those which are personal from those which are impersonal.

One trouble with most of these classification systems is that they are based on current and possibly temporary characteristics. On the other hand, division into telemedia and recording media is permanent because it is clearly an intrinsic differentiation. The ways in which a medium represents information define another basic and intrinsic set of characteristics. These ways are, basically, audio and visual, with the added possibility that the visual elements may be given motion.

For this book, we shall treat audio as a single element, although, in representing information, audio can be classified in three categories: (1) the human voice, which generally produces symbolic sound; (2) natural or artificial sounds and noises, which are largely concrete rather than symbolic; and (3) music, which is most often not a way of representing information; it is either a means of evoking emotional response, or an object in its own right.

Picture and print can be considered two ends of a visual continuum, ranging from highly realistic photographs in motion to static alphanumeric symbols. Between these extremes are drawings, diagrams, maps, charts, pictographs, ideograms, logograms and other symbols. The division between picture (icon) and print (symbol) in the above list occurs between the map and the chart. Despite the fact that a map may contain many symbolic elements, as a whole it is a kind of picture, since it represents something by expressing its spatial relationships. The chart, on the other hand, bears no relationship in physical form to the information it represents, except in a symbolic fashion. Hence, pictures are most appropriate for representing people, places and things; print is appropriate for generalities and for abstract concepts. Unless the latter function is performed by the spoken word, pictures, to be

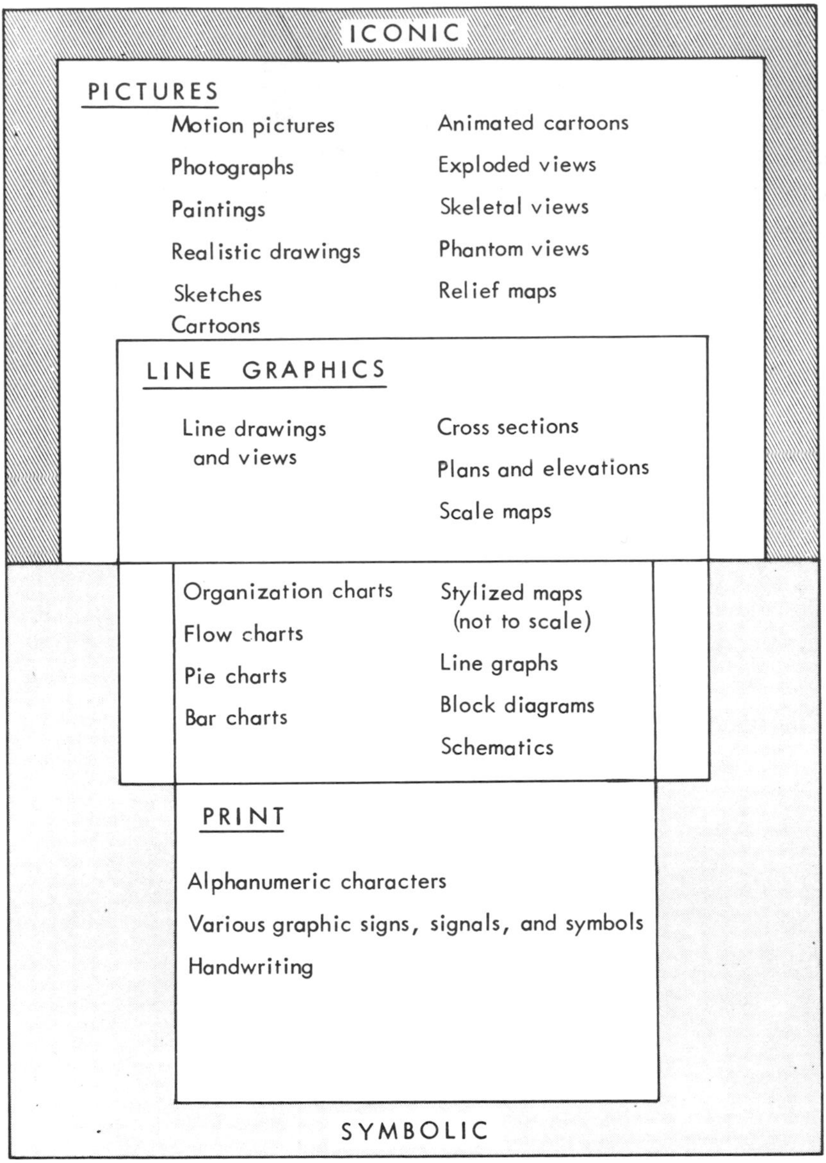

**ICONIC**

PICTURES

Motion pictures                Animated cartoons

Photographs                    Exploded views

Paintings                      Skeletal views

Realistic drawings             Phantom views

Sketches                       Relief maps

Cartoons

LINE   GRAPHICS

Line drawings                  Cross sections
and views
                               Plans and elevations

                               Scale maps

Organization charts            Stylized maps
                               (not to scale)
Flow charts
                               Line graphs
Pie charts
                               Block diagrams
Bar charts
                               Schematics

PRINT

Alphanumeric characters

Various graphic signs, signals, and symbols

Handwriting

SYMBOLIC

*Figure 8.* Visual means of representing information. Visual means that are iconic (having the character of an image) are shown in the top half of the figure; symbolic means in the bottom half. In the iconic section the more realistic means are listed, generally, toward the top. The area of line graphics includes both iconic and symbolic means, hence it overlaps both these areas. The list of means is representative, not exhaustive.

instructional, must almost always be accompanied by printed or written symbols.

For our present purposes, we shall divide the print-picture continuum into three parts instead of two, adding an intermediate class, line graphics. Under line graphics we will include all graphic representations that do not attempt to be realistic. Graphics that represent the three dimensions of space in a realistic manner will be considered pictures. All the known means of visual representation may be laid out in a continuum, extending from the most abstract at one end to the most realistic at the other (see Figure 8).

There are still other ways of representing information, such as Braille, which presents data to the tactile sense. A communication system has been developed* for men in combat which utilizes a pressure belt, applying meaningful pressures in various areas and in various patterns of pulses. These means of communication, however, are generally limited to special needs. Because of the relatively limited importance of the minor senses in comparison with sight and hearing, we can expect that tactile and pressure communication will not be extensively used.

The language of gesture and bodily demonstration, dramatization, mime and dance can also be highly useful in some situations. In the past, sign language has also been an important means of communication, used, for example, between American Indian tribes that were linguistically unrelated.

The ways of representing information used by the communication media listed in Table 1 are limited to the audio and the visual. The visual is further subdivided, as discussed above, into picture, line graphics and print. On this basis, then, seven classes of communication media are defined.

*Class I: Audio-Motion-Visual.* This is the most encompassing of all the media classes, since it utilizes all audio and visual means of representation. Television and sound film are Class I media.

---

*By HumRRO, Alexandria, Va.

Theoretically, programming for any of the other media may be transmitted or recorded by media of Class I.

*Class II: Audio-Still-Visual.* This is the second most encompassing media class; it is capable of everything that Class I media can do, except the representation of motion. Sound filmstrip is an example of Class II media.

*Class III: Audio-Semimotion.* Media of this class are called semimotion because they are capable of pointing and buildup but do not include the capacity to transmit or record full or realistic motion.

*Class IV: Motion-Visual.* This class is capable of everything included in Class I except audio. Silent film is the single current example of motion-visual media.

*Class V: Still-Visual.* Still-visual media represent information with all the visual methods, but do not represent motion, except by implication. The printed page and the filmstrip are examples of Class V media. It is the only class that is not time-based.

*Class VI: Audio.* Media using sound only, such as tape, disc and radio, comprise this class.

*Class VII: Print.* Media of Class VII represent information only through alphanumeric and other symbolic characters. Teletype and punched paper tape are the only current examples of telemedia and recording media in this class.


## MULTIMEDIA APPLICATIONS

The terms "multimedia" and "cross-media" can be considered synonymous; therefore, only the former will be used in this discussion. "Multimedia" applies to any situation where more than one medium is employed in a single communication. Multiple media can be used in either the sequential condition or the simultaneous. The most common pattern of multimedia use exists when several media are used sequentially as part of a single presentation. An auditorium program, for example, that begins with a tape recording, follows this with a filmstrip, and ends with a sound film is a multimedia presentation.

As an example of *simultaneous* multimedia presentation, audio or audiovisual media may be combined with printed materials, such as student workbooks, which are intended to be used while listening to the sound. It is necessary, of course, that the coordination of two such media be planned (and program materials for both be prepared and produced) together.

Most such simultaneous multimedia combinations include one of the still-visual media, the only class of media which is not time-based. The still-visual component, be it pictures or print, is generally "synchronized" to the progress of the time-based component (usually audio narration) by the viewer himself. This is to say, he turns pages as needed, looks where he is directed to look, and keeps up with the presentation.

A similar process takes place in the group mode in the case of radiovision or telelecture. During the audio presentation by radio or telephone, a projectionist listens for the proper cues, and advances slides in synchrony with the program.

It has been suggested that most useful multimedia combinations may in the future be integrated, resulting in systems that will have to be considered as discrete media. This is probably the route of most fruitful development in the media field. Various combinations of communication means will be tried out in practice, and those systems that prove most successful will be further developed—integrated, unified, simplified in operation and in program packaging—in response to demand. Many people believe that the most valuable of these new multimedia systems will be those constituting the communication components of computer controlled and managed instructional systems.

There is still another frequently used connotation to the term "multimedia": a presentation in which a lecturer uses several kinds of instructional *aids.* For example, the lecturer might use a portion of a tape-recorded speech as an object of study, a set of slides to illustrate his presentation, and a silent film over which he supplied a narration. While this would, in common parlance, be called a multimedia presentation, it might more properly be called a *multiaid* presentation. Since it is a single presentation in one time and place and not capable of being reproduced without the presence of the lecturer, it could not be called a medium of communication.

In recent years, for example, there has been a trend in media presentations toward the simultaneous display of several slides, or films and slides, on multiple screens. The projection function becomes so complex in these highly impressive presentations that the people who operate the projectors must often be the same people who have been involved in the production process. Several universities have permanently equipped auditoriums for the multiple-screen presentation of elaborately illustrated lectures. The screens are generally of the rear-projection type, forming a wall between the front of the auditorium and a projection room directly behind the screen(s). Several projectors are installed in this room; each is equipped with a short-focal-length lens in order to produce a large picture even though the projector-to-screen distance is very short. In a typical multimedia auditorium, a set of slides may be immediately followed by a film and this by a large-screen television image originating at the instructor's tele-vision camera, which is mounted over the lectern. The instructor uses this camera to display illustrations from books, to demon-strate small biological specimens, or to draw his own equations and diagrams. While the lecturer may display this series of instructional aids sequentially, the sophistication of the equipment and control system is such that all of the screens may be used simultaneously. A history professor, for example, may use a slide showing a map of the Ottoman Empire and a second slide listing a series of key events and dates, and he may leave these two displayed for constant reference while he runs another set of slides on the main screen.

Equipment is available on the open market with which it is possible to prepare a punched tape or audio tape for control purposes, on which the sequence of projectors and slides can be coded and controlled by push-button from the lectern. The instructor may follow a script and advance the projection system to the next event, however many projectors may be involved, simply by punching a single button whenever he reaches a cue to do so on his script.

Alternatively, he may depart from the preset procedure, controlling each projector manually if desired. Some installations include one or more random-access slide projectors, which make it possible for the instructor to return to any numbered slide for review or discussion, simply by pushing the correspondingly numbered button. It is even possible, in some of these installations, to prerecord the lecture on audio tape, add cue pulses in the proper places, and allow the audio tape to advance the control tape, which in turn operates the projectors and other instructional aids being used.

This example meets at least one of the criteria given earlier for an instructional medium: It is self-contained. It does not require, in the case of the recorded lecture at least, a live teacher's narration; it contains a complete program.

Even this recorded multimedia lecture, however, does not meet the second criterion—that programs produced in the medium must be capable of being reproduced. If it becomes common practice to package punched paper tape, slide sets and film clips along with recorded sound and ship the whole complex off to another location for a repeat of the presentation, then we can recognize a "multi-image" or "multi-image/multi-sound" medium. Most present multimedia installations are custom designed, and a presentation, once prepared and released, can generally be reproduced only in the auditorium for which it was designed.

It should be noted that approximately the same number of man-hours are required for the planning, preparation and rehearsal of such an auditorium presentation as are required to produce a program of the same length and containing the same elements in one of the Class I or Class II media. The costs of production equipment are also roughly similar. When this is recognized, it can be readily understood why some people have questioned the feasibility of the multimedia auditorium.

Of course, the multi-image presentation can be visually and emotionally most effective and a valuable enhancement for an institution. The display of a single-image audio-motion-visual or audio-still-visual medium suffers in comparison with multi-image projection. These current media can be recorded and distributed, however, and be extensively reproduced nearly anywhere, at many places at once, over a long period of time, at very little cost, and without any further concern on the part of the lecturer and his production assistants. Proponents may argue that the multimedia projection system and the reproducible medium are quite different things, which are appropriate for different purposes, at least at present—and cannot be considered alternatives for one another. This is true—the usual multimedia system is not yet a communication medium, but is simply a very sophisticated and dramatic method of automating the use of communication aids. But multi-image programming is becoming reproducible. There will be a period of chaos preceding standardization, as there is in the development of any medium. After this, something revolutionary may be expected.

Another multimedia development, the multimedia *device*, is beginning to make an appearance in the instructional field, the first example of which is the motion-still sound projector. Since a given program prepared for and presented by this device may consist of both audio-still-visual and audio-motion-visual segments, the system defies classification within the presently proposed taxonomy. Probably the best way to classify such a device at present is to call it a "multimedia system."

Separate sound is, of course, required, in the manner of the sound filmstrip devices which use audio tape; either the sound track itself or a parallel control track contains pulses which advance the projector from frame to frame, or cause it to run sequences of continuous motion. Motion picture projectors have long been capable of being halted on a still frame by the projectionist; many instructors have taken advantage of this feature to "freeze-frame" a motion sequence when additional time was desired to discuss or study the picture. Until the appearance of the motion-still projector, however, still frames could only be obtained manually—they could not be programmed.

The combination still and motion system permits considerable savings in film stock, since still sequences such as titles or static scenes need be represented by only one (or in some systems several) frames each. Evidence shows that for many decades the average instructional film has incorporated relevant motion in less than half its length.\* Motion picture films, accordingly, may be specially printed for still-motion projection at a saving of over half of the film stock and associated costs.

It is also possible, at least with proposed motion-still equipment, to use the same visual sequence for a second purpose by providing a different sound and control component. Thus a film prepared for doctors might also be used for nurses by halting on different frames as needed for a different verbal presentation.

It has been noted previously that the trend in instruction is toward the individual mode of use for communication media. Films, tapes, sound filmstrips and combination media will in the future be *studied,* not merely screened. This means that the capability to fast-forward or partially rewind a program, an action analogous to referring ahead or reviewing in a book, will be increasingly important.

At present, only one separate-sound device (proposed by Kinelogic, a subsidiary of Dictaphone) is capable of maintaining synchrony between sound and still picture after fast-forwarding or partial rewinding. (The sound-on-slide devices and sound page are, of course, capable of this, but they are not as yet competitive with filmstrip, motion picture, etc., for large-scale distribution.)

Later generations of motion-still equipment, capable of maintaining synchrony under any conditions of use without

---

\*Keislar, in 1945, studied 24 science films and found that about 45 percent of all film footage contained no motion at all, while the remainder portrayed much movement that was insignificant to the apparent learning objectives. He stated, "Evidence suggests that less than half of the total footage contained in instructional films depicts motion significantly contributing to desired learning." Similar studies by McClusky (1924), O'Conner (1942) and Irwin (1950) produced similar conclusions.[6]

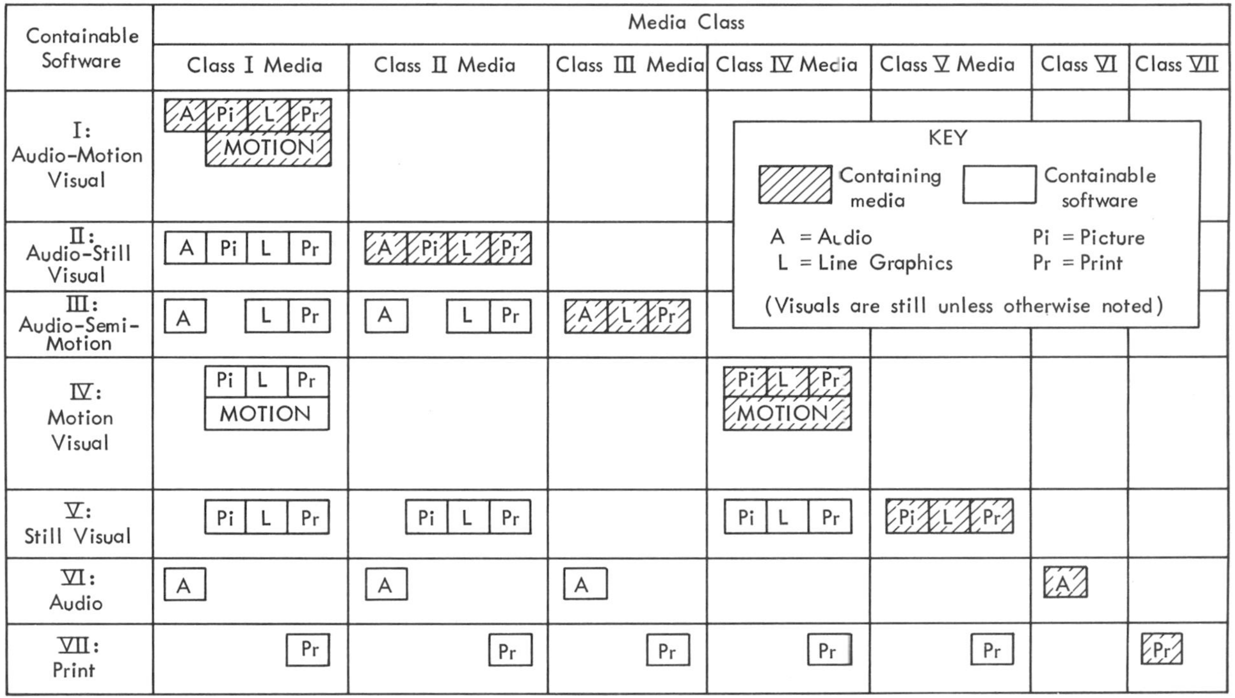

Media Class

| Containable Software | Class I Media | Class II Media | Class III Media | Class IV Media | Class V Media | Class VI | Class VII |
|---|---|---|---|---|---|---|---|
| I: Audio-Motion Visual | A/Pi/L/Pr MOTION *(hatched)* | | | | | | |
| II: Audio-Still Visual | A Pi L Pr | A/Pi/L/Pr *(hatched)* | | | | | |
| III: Audio-Semi-Motion | A L Pr | A L Pr | A/L/Pr *(hatched)* | | | | |
| IV: Motion Visual | Pi L Pr MOTION | | | Pi/L/Pr MOTION *(hatched)* | | | |
| V: Still Visual | Pi L Pr | Pi L Pr | | Pi L Pr | Pi/L/Pr *(hatched)* | | |
| VI: Audio | A | A | A | | | A *(hatched)* | |
| VII: Print | Pr | Pr | Pr | Pr | Pr | | Pr *(hatched)* |

KEY

Containing media *(hatched box)*    Containable software *(plain box)*

A = Audio    Pi = Picture
L = Line Graphics    Pr = Print

(Visuals are still unless otherwise noted)

*Figure 9.* Media within media. Each column represents a class of media and is headed by a set of symbols indicating the ways of representing information characteristic of that class. Below in each column are indicated the classes of program software which can be contained (transmitted or recorded). Specific media within each of these classes are described in Chapter 5.

having to start the program over again at the beginning, will greatly extend the usefulness of communication media in instruction.

## MEDIA WITHIN MEDIA

A primary advantage of a classification based on ways of representing information is that it indicates very readily how the program software of one medium may form the content or recording medium for another. The most common example is the transmission of film via television, or conversely, the recording of a television program on film. Figure 9 shows how program software of simpler media may be included in more complex media. For example, a Class V recording such as a filmstrip (line V) could be transmitted or recorded by media in columns I, II, IV or V. Class I media, it can readily be seen, may record or transmit, as the case may be, program materials from any of the other media classes. These relationships are theoretical; practical application would depend on various technical considerations. For example, the levels of fidelity of the two media must match.

Standard television, for example, is not capable of very high definition and probably as a result tends to be viewed, at least in schools, from about twice the distance from which films and slides are viewed, relative to screen size. Thus no more than ten lines of print with no more than 40 character spaces per line are certain to be readable. This amounts to less than 400 character spaces at best, assuming the corners are usable and the receiver is not truncating the picture at the edges.

If a standard page, containing some 2500 characters, is to be transmitted via a television system, either the page must be retyped so the lines are 40 characters in length instead of 80, and are transmitted, in effect, as several pages, or a high-definition television system must be used. Also, program software must be compatible. Silent film, recorded at its standard 16-frames-per-second rate, for instance, may be transmitted by television, but must be run, generally, on TV sound film projection equipment, operating at half again that speed. The result is a speeding up of motion, unless either (1) the silent footage is originally shot at 24 frames per second, or (2) it is projected into the television system at the slower speed.

## MOTION

There are several kinds of motion, some of which are possible in media classes in which no motion component is listed. Motion, in this discussion, is used to mean the representation of full and continuous movement, the way it is perceived in reality. Motion is applicable to all visual elements in a display, singly, separately, or in concert. Camera movement, such as panning, tilting, or zooming on still pictures is motion. Full animation is motion; semi-animation, where the position of objects changes abruptly, is not. Full animation can only be accomplished in a Class I or Class IV medium.

Class II media are capable of some types of simple animation of simulated motion, such as rapid picture sequence (from a second or two each up to several per second). If all elements but one in a sequence of two pictures are identical, and if the one element which changes does not change too much, the effect will be perceived or at least interpreted as movement. The motion of a man pumping up a tire, for example, might be simulated indefinitely by simply cutting back and forth between two still pictures showing him in the two extreme positions. However, not all Class II hardware is capable of such rapid picture change.

Still-visual media, Class V, have no time dimension (i.e., they do not play or run at a set rate as motion or audio media do). However, they are still capable of implying motion in several ways. Some of these are symbolic, such as "whiz lines" trailing after an object in the direction opposite to its movement. The representation of subjects in dynamic disequilibrium is also frequently used to imply motion.

The adding of new elements to a visual display can also contribute a kind of motion, e.g., (1) pop-on labels, or (2) underlining or circling. Labels can be made to suddenly appear by cutting from one still picture to another in which all elements are identical except the added label.

Telewriting is capable of another type of motion. A line can be drawn by a moving stylus; and element by element, writing and/or graphic representations take form. This has the same pedagogic advantage as the chalkboard: items are displayed gradually, as they are needed. For the purpose of this discussion, however, the process is called "build-up," not motion. It is indicated on the classification (Table 1) by a smaller than normal x. Underlining and circling may be done readily with telewriting.

There is still another type of motion, which might be called "pointing," of which telewriting is again a good example. Pointing, whether it is done by means of the moving stylus, as in telewriting, or electronically by a spot, oblong, or arrow superimposed on the screen, leaves no record and contributes in no permanent way to the display.

A future form of electronic transmission might consist of still-picture television plus an electronic pointer controlled live at the point of origination. Signals to locate and move this pointer would be fairly simple to transmit, and should require little additional transmission channel space. A combination of telewriting with slow-scan television would be the next logical development. This could be capable of writing and build-up as well as still-visual display, when presented on a television system.

It has been shown in several research studies that full motion is not needed in the majority of instructional presentations and may even be a distraction in some. As we have noted, several studies have indicated that significant or germane motion constitutes only a minor part of instructional films. Most of the motion in such films adds realism to photographed action or adds a dynamic quality to otherwise static material. In other words, so far as cognitive learning is concerned, it is motion largely for its own sake. (Possibly, there may be behavioral changes in the affective domain, attained by such motion, which have so far escaped measurement.)

In the light of this information, then, it is surprising to see relatively little use being made of audio-still-visual (Class II) media, especially since they are *very* much less expensive media in terms of the costs of recording and of transmission by wire or wireless.

## THE ROLE OF COMPUTERS AS INSTRUCTIONAL MEDIA

The reader may have wondered why computers have not been listed among the communication media, especially since they are beginning to show such promise in the area of instruction. The reason is that *computers are basically control and computation systems; they are not communication systems.* For example, information presentation is one of the functions involved in computer assisted instruction; whether this involves audio or visual materials, or simply type, it is performed by one of the communication media acting as a component of the total computer system. Computers are also being used increasingly simply to control information-transmission systems, such as teletype, or such as radio and television broadcasting stations.

Some educators who have investigated the growing field of computer assisted instruction (CAI) propose that the computer is potentially capable of tremendous flexibility and can be combined with and/or integrated into so many instructional media that it will be capable of executing nearly all instructional functions. There is also strong evidence to indicate that the computer will be able to perform some of these functions far better than they have ever been performed by any other means, machine or human. These are strong statements, but these are rapidly changing times. Today many people expect that small electronic machines will be capable of *simultaneously* custom-tailoring instruction for hundreds or even thousands of different learners with different, changing needs. Cost constraints, though serious today, may be ameliorated by a continuing decrease in the cost of central processing units and the development of inexpensive terminals and other peripheral equipment.

Instruction by a computer system is admittedly still in a primitive phase. In this discussion we are looking ahead—very far ahead, in the opinion of some. The first communication medium to be widely used by computers for presenting information to the learner was the teletype or the electric typewriter. This is expected, since type was all that could be displayed by most of the existing computer terminal equipment. Besides, the print medium can handle both specific and abstract information on practically any subject matter. Experimental projects and laboratory demonstrations, however, have indicated that at least ten different communication media can be associated with a computer, and in any desired combination.*

On the presentation side, an increasing number of systems now incorporate a cathode-ray tube (CRT), on which print can be made to appear much faster than the teletype can produce it. Some of these systems can also display various types of computer-generated graphics. Other systems have an audio component, which uses prerecorded audio tapes; these systems are particularly useful in language teaching. Systems are in use which generate their own audible speech, which has (at the present state of the art) a somewhat artificial quality, and is as impersonal as printed words in a book, but which actually can be created especially by the computer for the specific dialogue at hand. Other systems can display visual materials such as slides, microfiche and the like, which are selected by the computer from a file of recorded materials stored within the individual terminal. Some of these consoles also store motion-picture materials for similar control and display.

An almost equal number of devices now exist that allow the learner to respond to the computer. The teletype, the electric

---

*i.e., TV, still TV, teletype, sound film, video tape, film TV recording, recorded still TV, sound filmstrip, sound slide-set and audio tape.

typewriter, Engelbart's five-finger typewriter* and the touchtone phone are devices by which the learner can respond in print. Cathode-ray tube display devices make possible the display of graphic material, and several systems allow the learner to respond by pointing to a spot or area in the graphic display (e.g., the light pen, the stylus of the Rand Tablet** and the finger on a touch-sensitive screen).

Then there are several possible ways in which a learner, in future computer instruction, may construct his own graphic response. The Rand Tablet, coupled with character recognition, allows the user to at least print, if not to write in script. Using the Rand Tablet stylus, he may make line drawings, which are then recorded according to the coordinate points that the stylus has located. For drawing, the stylus or light pen is superior to devices such as the "joy-stick" and the "tracking ball" which were previously used for two-dimensional pointing and simple lines. An esoteric new device is the Engelbart mouse, a box the size of a large mouse trailing a wire tail. When the operator moves the mouse about on the surface of an ordinary table, a pair of wheels on the underside of the creature register the amount of motion in each of the two dimensions, and a moving spot or "bug" is displayed on the cathode-ray tube. Most of these graphic-response techniques were designed for the purpose of generating materials, not for instructing. There is a long step yet to take between the present stage of development and that where a learner will no longer be constrained in the type of response he may make, and where the computer will be able to understand and evaluate the response sufficiently that it can act intelligently upon it.

In the distant future, beyond a doubt, machines will be able to understand and respond to human speech in some constrained language. An interface device by which one may converse with a

---

*Developed by Douglas Engelbart, Stanford Research Institute.

**A surface about a foot square on which the user may make writing and drawing movements with a stylus. The results of this action are recorded and simultaneously displayed on a cathode-ray screen.

computer in ordinary human language, instead of specially designed human-machine-interface languages is considered much farther away, if it can be developed at all.

In addition to live-response media, recording techniques such as simple paper-and-pencil methods are also being integrated with computer instruction. For example, in some applications the computer may be used for batch processing—correcting papers overnight, so to speak—and feeding back knowledge of results the next day.

Considering only the presentation and response methods listed here, and assuming a combination of only one method of presentation and one method of response, a total of some 70 or more different stimulus-response systems are possible. If we assume what is even more likely, that in any one device several methods of display will be combined with several methods of response, *the total of possible combinations of the presently known presentation and response systems is well over a thousand.*

Thus, the development of computer instruction systems will not be constrained simply by lack of possibilities. The most important aspect of the computer's capability for directing learner response is that the computer, when properly programmed, can react to the learner's response in a highly discriminating and complex fashion—much more so than ordinary teaching machines—in providing knowledge of results and altering both information presentation and direction of activities in accordance with the learner's needs. The computer can base these decisions not only on the correctness of the learner's responses to criterion questions, but also on data such as his rate of improvement and the time it takes him to answer correctly. It may also take various exogenous factors (e.g., sex, age, socioeconomic background) into account when they are relevant.

The administration of exams by computer appears to offer very great advantages, not only in evaluation of a learner's achievement after instruction, but also in diagnosing the state of his knowledge and capabilities before instruction. Media are of course *used by* the computer for the presentation of information and response stimuli, but the computer itself is much more than a communication medium.

The computer may adapt an examination while it is being administered, instantly evaluating the student's answers and basing the selection of a second question on the student's answer to the first. The most comprehensive question, or problem, may be presented first; if the student handles this satisfactorily he may be considered competent and need no further questions on that area. If not, the computer may probe with further questions to diagnose his state of knowledge. Thus each student may, in effect, be given a different exam.

The purpose of the examination is thus broadened; instead of being merely a test sample of the student's capability, the exam becomes a diagnosis of his abilities and weaknesses, and a valuable aid to future tutoring and counseling.

Interaction—the opportunity to discuss a subject with one's peers or with someone who knows more about it—has traditionally been accomplished through classroom discussion, led or at least controlled by a teacher. It is conceivable, however, that a computer-controlled instructional system could do some rather complex things within this function. Dialogue between learner and program has been demonstrated in a limited number of expensively produced programs. This will develop much further. It is possible for the computer to interconnect, at appropriate points in a program, two or more learners of the same achievement level. For example, if a computer system has 10,000 terminals, as one study has proposed,[7] it might be possible to find two or more learners at or near the same place in the same program, at the same moment. The computer could give them a point to argue, or have them play as opponents in some kind of simulation game. This kind of interaction, in the individual mode, might actually be more effective than classroom discussion, since the computer learner would be likely to participate 100 percent of the time.

There are important functions of the instructional process which a computer probably never will be able to perform as well as a human. One of these is the evaluation of unanticipated learner responses, and another is personal attention. Here, humanists believe that the machine can have little effectiveness. There is evidence, however, that even the one-way broadcasting media give people the feeling they have friends and acquaintances coming into the house, and children feel a strong sense of being *liked* by a beloved television personality. It is possible to conceive of even closer and more intense surrogate relationships developing from a program that is highly individual and personal in its response to the learner. Even today, the feeling of personal attention that a learner derives from a good computer program may well be far in excess of that experienced in the usual impersonal college lecture course.

# 5.

# Communication Media: Individual Descriptions

In this section, all of the currently used media, plus the new or laboratory-stage media which may have application soon, are described and discussed, with emphasis on instructional applications and implications.

## CLASS I: AUDIO-MOTION-VISUAL MEDIA

Class I (audio-motion-visual) is the universal, all-inclusive class of media. It includes sound film television and the various means of recording television. There are no ways of representing reality in any of the other media classes of which Class I is not also capable. This is to say that there is no combination of audio and visual elements that can be organized into a program for any of the other media which cannot, given the proper interface equipment, be recorded or transmitted by means of one of the audio-motion-visual media (see Figure 9, page 78). Such procedures might be impractical and wasteful, but they would be possible. Class V still-visual media alone have capabilities that Class I media do not possess, because still-visual media are not time-based.

## Television

Television is the most universal of all the telecommunication media in that it combines more ways of representing information than any other; it is also the most heavily used in education today. A 1967 estimate placed the number of elementary and secondary school learners in the United States who receive a small part of their instruction through television at 10 million—about 20 percent of the children enrolled in these grade levels. In practice, many uses of television do not require or utilize its full spectrum of possibilities. It has been frequently pointed out that a given program could have been done as well by some less complex or less expensive medium: a music program by radio, a blackboard lecture by telewriting, etc. The most convincing of such observations concerns the nascent still-TV medium and the extent to which it might replace or supplement television in education. Several studies have been noted which indicate that instructional films make very little use of relevant motion,[8] and the same is probably also true of instructional television. It is possible that still-TV media will be able to convey over 60 percent of the cognitive stimuli we now convey via full television; some estimates have ranged as high as 85 percent.

However, it is not always necessary to use the full capabilities of a medium 100 percent of the time (if indeed, it were even desirable), in order to justify its operational costs. Now that a wide spectrum of media is available, which can be totally embraced by a local school district, a medical college, or a local consortium of schools of any type, the possibilities of choice are becoming apparent. It is only when at least one completely justifiable use for television calls on its full potentials—sound, print, picture, motion and the immediacy of live transmission—that television can be applied successfully as a universal instructional medium. Under such conditions, a television system can be utilized for any telecommunication purpose, in full or partial modes, audio only, still pictures only, or simply as a transmission medium to distribute recorded materials.

Before the development of video tape (approximately 1956),

television recording was dependent on kinerecordings, which were, even at best, easily distinguishable from live transmission because of their degraded quality. Entertainment television was primarily a live medium in those days; but since the appearance of video tape, which at its best is difficult to distinguish from live transmission, even after many generations of duplication, the television mass medium has become primarily a means of transmitting films and video tape recordings. A few instructional television systems have continued to transmit their programs live, however. Both the Anaheim (California) City School District and the Washington County (Maryland) systems are based primarily on live television. The necessity for producing lessons afresh each time they are transmitted (each year in these cases) has the advantage of encouraging frequent revision, and tends to allay television teachers' fears that they might some day be replaced with the products of their own creativity. Until recently, the cost of equipment and the large stock of 2-inch tape required for the storage of all of a televised course made the extensive use of video tape impractical. At Anaheim, for example, some 1440 lessons are produced and transmitted yearly to the third, fourth and fifth grades. At $100 per hour for the standard broadcast video tape stock they use (running at half speed), the backlog of tape alone would cost $144,000 and would require some 300 linear feet of shelf space. The development of less expensive, smaller-gauge tape equipment cut these costs nearly in half, and recently they have been halved again, but picture degradation still limits the usefulness of the narrowest, least expensive tape systems. Video tape, however, is used frequently for delayed transmission, erased and used again the following day. If delayed transmission (1 hour to as much as 48 hours, in some instances) is considered to be the transmission of a recording medium instead of live television, then live television is today a relatively small part of instructional television. And, indeed, instructional television must be considered largely a transmitting system, rather than a telecommunication medium.

Broadcast television has been regulated and standardized in

all countries, and although there are several different sets of standards in the world, in general all broadcast television in any one country is of one type, and all of any one country's transmitting and receiving equipment is compatible. This holds true even between monochrome and color, i.e., color programs can be received on black and white sets and monochrome programs may be displayed in black and white on color receivers.

Most closed-circuit television in this country follows the established broadcast standards: 525 scanning lines per frame at a rate of 30 frames per second, utilizing a 6-MHz bandwidth for transmission. This makes it possible for many television system components to be used for both broadcast and closed-circuit applications; closed-circuit television can use off-the-shelf equipment at minimum cost. However, many closed-circuit applications require higher definition quality and broader bandwidths for transmission. Such systems require special components from one end to the other and are incompatible with the standard 525-line equipment. Because of the extra cost of such equipment, and its incompatibility with standard systems, it has not been used widely in instruction. A few installations of high-definition television (up to 1500 scanning lines) are to be found in medical schools, however.

### Picturephone

Picturephone, a development of the Bell Telephone Company, is now being placed into regular service. To date, it has been demonstrated for various periods between Disneyland and whatever World's Fair happened to be in operation, as a public-relations exhibit for the telephone company. A regular service has been operating since 1963 between fixed booths in New York, Washington and Chicago.

The terminal equipment consists of a small combination monitor/camera with a screen about 5 x 7 inches in size, the longer dimension being the vertical, perhaps to keep it from being thought of as a television system. Since the image quality is not equal to that of small-screen television, such comparison is to be discouraged. Picturephone uses a bandwidth about one-sixth that of standard television, so it should be very much less costly to transmit. Even at that, the bandwidth required is about that of some 250 standard 4-KHz telephone channels.

To extend the usefulness of Picturephone, the Model II Picturephone set has been provided with a small mirror in front of the lens to direct the camera's view downward. The user may hinge this mirror into place whenever he wishes to transmit graphic or pictorial material or his own writing or drawing. He may change the field of view over a 2-to-1 range by electronically zooming in or out, and he may change the camera focus to transmit scenes containing two or more people up to 20 feet away.

The Picturephone has been conceived primarily as a means of adding vision to the telephone conversation. (In the 1920's, whenever television was discussed, this is the form people imagined that it would take.) It is essentially a television system, in that it may transmit sound, print, picture and motion in real time, but in its present form it has such low definition in comparison with standard video systems that it could not readily be used for the same purposes.

If Picturephone is to be used for instructional purposes, it will be in the individual mode, possibly connected with an on-line computer system with both video and audio coming from some future digital memory device. Picturephone may present advantages over telephone instruction in achieving affective objectives, since the presentation would be more personal, with both the instructor's voice and facial expressions coming into the play. Of course, improved transmission techniques may increase the picture definition, and a somewhat larger screen may become possible; with these improvements, the medium's usefulness in instruction will be increased accordingly.

If installation of a Picturephone in the home eventually becomes practical and popular, its use as an individual-mode instructional device will probably follow. The convenience of receiving tutorial instructional presentations, of practicing skills, of testing and evaluating one's progress from the home, office, or study carrel, especially if this instruction is computer managed, may be one of the most important advantages of Picturephone.

### Sound Film

Sound film is to the recording media what television is to the telemedia, a universal medium embracing all three methods of representing information—sound, picture, and print—and capable of investing the visual elements, where appropriate, with motion. Sound film as a mass medium is now some 40 years old, and it has lived through one crisis where it seemed that television might replace it, and another where it seemed that television production techniques and video tape recording might at least replace the motion-picture camera and associated studio techniques. The latter issue has not been settled, but merely deferred, pending further advancement in the electronic art.

Sound film began as a separate-sound medium; the sound was distributed on a large disc and synchronized in playback with the film. Sound-on-film was quickly developed, however, and the successful development of sound film into a mass medium was doubtlessly dependent on this feature. Had sound film consisted of Vitaphone discs synchronized with otherwise silent film, it might never have overcome the limitations of dependence on human factors in the transport and projection processes. Damage to film prints could not have been repaired simply by splicing out the bad portions, which is the current practice, without destroying sound-picture synchrony. This point is made because some new separate-sound film techniques are now making an appearance. While inexpensive in comparison with sound-on-film, these methods suffer from the same limitations as the early Vitaphone movies.

Sound-film standards were originally based on the use of 35mm film running at a speed of 24 frames per second. The sound track was optical, consisting of a strip of variable area or variable density which, on passing through a projector, transferred this photographic analog of sound into electrical impulses by modulating the beam of an exciter lamp falling on a photocell. Within five years or so, sound-on-film was also added to 16mm film, again with a film speed of 24 frames per second, although when expressed in inches this only amounted to 7.2 inches per second instead of the 18 inches per second of the larger-frame 35mm film.

In the middle sixties, 8mm film acquired sound; and, when Super 8 was developed, it acquired sound as well. This development had been delayed until higher-quality recording techniques were devised, and improvements were made in film emulsion. The 8mm sound film contains 80 frames per foot, which runs at 3.6 inches per second; Super 8, at 72 frames per foot, runs at 4 inches per second. In comparison with current audio tape speeds, this should be sufficient speed to obtain adequate quality, as indeed both Cine-8* and Super 8 exhibit in practice.

Film may carry optical sound, in which case the sound track is composed of the same photographic emulsion as the picture portion of the film, or the sound track may be magnetic. In the latter case, a magnetic-oxide strip is added to the film, usually after the picture has already been processed. The sound is recorded on this track, using conventional magnetic recording procedures. Magnetic sound on film became available soon after the introduction of magnetic tape recording, and essentially replaced optical sound on 35mm film. It has been threatening to do the same in 16mm film, but progress is slow.

The development of 8mm and Super 8 sound film was accompanied by another significant device, the 8mm-sound cartridge projector. Silent loop cartridges had been introduced by Technicolor in 1961; two years later Fairchild introduced the first sound loop cartridge. By the end of the decade there were at least ten manufacturers offering continuous-loop sound cartridges and projectors, each operating with different standards or cartridge shapes so that one manufacturer's cartridge would not fit another's projector. Even the Super 8 film within the cartridges was not interchangeable. Some carried magnetic sound tracks,

---

*Cine-8 is the technical term for the original 8mm format sometimes called regular or standard 8.

some optical; sound was placed as far as 120 frames in advance of the image for some cartridges, and as far as 28 frames in retard for others. At this writing there appears to be a growing industry-wide effort to standardize these loop cartridges, using magnetic sound with an advance of eighteen frames. The cartridge projector is proving very popular because it eliminates the need for the skill of projector operation, the lack of which in many teachers and students has in the past discouraged the use of film in classrooms and made it impractical to consider using films in the individual mode.

Another type of film cartridge and projector has also made its appearance and seems to have several advantages over the loop cartridge. This second type will be referred to here as the "supply-reel cartridge," although its originator, Eastman Kodak, calls it a reel-to-reel cartridge.* In this design, the cartridge is really no more than a simple means of covering and protecting the supply reel. In operation, the film feeds into the machines and onto a take-up reel. It never completely leaves the supply reel, however, to which it is permanently anchored at the tail end. At the end of a screening the film rewinds quickly into the cartridge. The supply-reel cartridge design is also used in the EVR system (see page 98).

The supply-reel cartridge has important advantages over the continuous-loop type. To begin with, the film can be moved backward as well as forward. It can be very frustrating to the user of a 20-minute loop film to miss one key word and not be able to hear it again until he reaches the same point again on a second running. In addition to the possibility of movement in both directions, some of the projectors for the supply-reel cartridge are incorporating fast-forward and fast-reverse features, thus providing

---

*In this discussion the term "reel-to-reel cartridge" will be reserved for a cartridge that, like the audio cassette, incorporates both supply and take-up reels within the cartridge. The supply-reel cartridge, like conventional film projectors, is also a reel-to-reel *system.* Only the loop cartridge is not. In general, the term "cassette" will be used for the reel-to-reel *cartridge,* whether it contains audio or visual material.

for film a degree of accessibility which has long been characteristic of audio- and video-tape machines. The projector design determines this feature as well as the cartridge. Since fast film movement through a loop cartridge is impossible, fast forward or reverse is only possible in those designs based on the supply-reel or the cassette principle.

As with any equipment, added complexity brings added operational problems. During the 1960's, as a transitional stage before the cartridge projector, manufacturers offered many self-threading models, hoping to reduce the difficulty that unskilled people experience in operating projectors. The self-threading projectors, however, often caused even skilled projectionists added headaches. If the film being projected is new, and without splices, these projectors generally work well. The average film, however, is less than ideal, and if a splice should open while the film is in the inaccessible self-threading works of the machine, the machine will sometimes continue running until the works are jammed with crumpled film. In the cartridge projectors, where the film is even more inaccessible, splices are almost totally banned. This means that cartridge projection is not suitable for local production where original film is used, containing the splices that result from editing.

An inexpensive system of sound-film production for the home was offered by Bell and Howell in 1968. This is a separate-sound system; the picture is recorded by a silent Super 8 camera while sound is recorded by a small cassette tape recorder carried by the cameraman on a shoulder strap. Camera and tape recorder are synchronized by pulses generated by the camera and recorded on the tape; during projection, these same pulses control the projector speed and keep sound and picture in synchrony. Synchronex offers similar equipment, and a service which transfers the separate sound onto a magnetic track on the picture film. The resulting sound-on-film is then projected by means of a standard Super 8 sound projector.

While schools constitute the largest market for 16- and 8-mm film projectors, business and industry are by far the greatest buyers of motion-picture software. In 1968, school systems accounted for 65 percent of the sales of motion-picture projectors; other user systems in the fields of business, government, community agencies, medicine and health, and religion made up the remainder.* Business and industry accounted for only 19 percent of the money spent. In the purchase of software, however, business and industry accounted for 53 percent and schools only 22 percent of the total of $454 million spent. It is interesting to note that total software expenditures in this medium exceeded hardware by almost eight to one. In schools it was less than three to one, but in industry it exceeded twenty to one.

By way of comparison it may be noted that when the totals of all other audiovisual hardware and software are compared, *hardware* was the greatest market by one and one-half to one in the schools and two to one in industry. Of course, this includes many communication aid devices, particularly the overhead transparency projector, for which software is generally produced locally.

### Film Television Recording

The first method to be used for recording television programs involved simply photographing the face of a television receiver with a motion-picture camera. Because the tube in a television receiver is known as a kinescope tube, recording of the visual image it displays is known as kinescope recording. The term is often shortened to "kinerecording," and the resulting film is commonly called a "kinescope" or "kine."

When a kinerecording is made from a video tape recording rather than a live broadcast, the process is, of course, the same, but it is then called "tape-to-film transfer."

It is entirely possible to photograph any receiver screen with almost any kind of movie camera, but the asynchrony between the 30 frames per second of television and the 24 frames per second of

---

*Hope, Thomas W. "Market Review: Nontheatrical Film and Audio-Visual—1968," *Journal of the SMPTE, Vol. 78, No. 11,* November 1969, pp. 973-988.

sound film may cause roll or flicker unless the camera is equipped with a special shutter. The best kinerecorders consist of a camera specially made for the purpose, plus a kinescope tube of special sharpness, color and luminosity, mounted together on a rigid base.

Kinerecording was first done commercially in 1947, strictly for record-keeping, but it rapidly came to be depended on for rebroadcast purposes, and for program syndication between stations that were not yet interconnected by live means. At one point it was estimated that kinerecording consumed something like six times as much film stock as the entire motion-picture industry. This came to a rather abrupt end, however, with the appearance of video tape.

Since video tape was far superior to kinerecording in picture quality, and could be reused many times, while film stock could be recorded on only once, it was expected that kinerecording would disappear. This did not occur, however; then its demise was again predicted nearly 10 years later, when low-cost portable video tape machines costing less than many sound-film projectors became available. These predictions were still not realized, however; quite to the contrary, the greatest developments in the art and science of kinescope recording have taken place since the advent of video tape.

There are several reasons for the importance of kinerecording in instruction. To begin with, permanent storage of program material can be less expensive on film than on standard broadcast video tape. Kinescope recordings, which are on standard 16mm film stock, may be projected wherever a 16mm sound projector and screen can be set up. All that is required beyond this equipment is standard 110-volt electrical current, a semi-darkened room or a rear-projection cabinet and a projector operator. Video tape, on the other hand, requires a television monitor for display and, generally, a system to distribute the television signal from a central point of playback to individual viewing locations. In many schools, especially in the Armed Forces, the use of kinerecordings is the most practical alternative because so many sound-film projectors already exist.

Kinerecording was first done only on 16mm film; later, a higher quality was obtained with 35mm film, which the television networks used for program delay and rebroadcast before the development of video tape. Experiments have been made with 8mm and Super 8 kinescope recording, and at least one model of a Super 8 kinescope recorder is now on the market. This system performs a function that is certain to be used extensively in the future: the transfer of video tapes to Super 8 cartridge form for use in the individual mode.

Kinescope recording is a complex process involving many decoding/encoding transfer stages as the picture proceeds from one medium to another. In live television, pictorial information exists as electrical impulses. The kinescope tube transfers these to visual patterns of light and shade. The kinescope recording camera picks up these variations of light, and places their images on a film emulsion, where they are transferred to variations in chemical change, which are subsequently made permanent by the developing process.

When a kinerecording is subsequently transmitted via a television system, it must go through two more transfer stages, from photochemistry to optics as it is projected into a television camera, and from optics to electronics when the camera tube scans out the picture.

Video tape owes its higher quality on retransmission largely to the fact that it is not necessary to go from electrical signals through an optical process to photographic recording and back again. In video tape recording, television signals are transferred to patterns of magnetization in the tape emulsion, and these are, on playback, transferred directly back to television signals.

A new approach to television film recording is exemplified by electron beam recording (EBR), which short-cuts the encoding/decoding process of kinescope recording by eliminating the initial optical stage. The video signal, in EBR, is not formed into an image on a cathode-ray tube and photographed on motion-picture film. Instead, video is implanted directly onto the film itself without going through the optical stage. The film runs in a vacuum chamber, where a moving electron beam scans the picture onto each successive frame of continuously moving film. From this point on, the process is the same as in other types of television film recording.

### Electronic Video Recording

Electronic video recording (EVR) is a method of recording images and sound on motion-picture film, using the previously described EBR method of recording. At the time that it appeared, EVR was the most highly miniaturized film system, forming images about 4 millimeters in width (Super 8 images are 6 millimeters wide). Proposed cost schedules indicated that EVR would also be the most inexpensive recording method of all the Class I media.

The EVR recording system can accept input from any of the Class I media. Output display, however, is exclusively by means of a television system. Optical projection equipment has neither been developed nor contemplated. Thus, EVR differs basically from other film television recording systems in that it is a method of making film recordings especially for television use, rather than a method of recording television on film for other uses.

In practice, the producer who wishes to distribute materials in the EVR form will produce his program on film or video tape, then send it to a laboratory for transfer to EVR. The program will be returned in supply-reel cartridge form. In addition to television receivers, users must have EVR playback units, which will cost, to begin with, about the same as sound motion-picture projectors (approximately $800); a second-generation consumer product is expected to reach the market within a year or two, which may cost only half this much.

The EVR process involves the use of a very slow and very fine-grain 35mm motion-picture film stock, manufactured in England by the Ilford Company. The producer's original film or video tape is transferred to a 35mm master negative on this stock, in eight parallel strips of tiny images. From this EVR master, release prints can be run off by contact printing at the rate of a half-hour program every 30 seconds—about the time it takes to press an LP record. The films are then split into four strips, each 8.75 millimeters wide, containing two tracks. Seven hundred and fifty feet of master 35mm film, which ordinarily would run for a little over 8 minutes on a theater screen, holds 4 hours of EVR material.

A 7-inch-diameter EVR cartridge will contain an hour's program on its two tracks. After a half-hour of screening, the film is rewound (1-minute rewind time) and the second track is run. It is possible to move back and forth between the two tracks, sampling each at will, a possible mode of use in some future programmed-instruction application. Sacrificing sound, one may stop on a still frame at any point and move, frame by frame, either forward or backward by means of a manual control.

Magnetic sound tracks accompany each track of images along the outer edge of the film. A series of what look like sprocket holes runs down the center of the film, one at each frame line. They are not perforated, however; control is achieved optically, so loss of synchrony does not mean torn film.

Color EVR is scheduled to appear first on the home market. It will require twice as much film area as black and white; the first track of each pair will carry a black and white image, while the second track will carry the color information, also in black and white.* Color EVR cartridges will, of course, contain only a half-hour of program rather than an hour.


### Holographic Recording

With the invention of the laser, a light source consisting of very coherent, highly monochromatic light, many new developments have become possible which will affect the future of communication media. Probably the first will be the hologram.

A hologram is a recorded image based on the principle of light interference. The usual hologram, held in the hand, looks

---

*CBS, now marketing EVR, points out that this kind of color is not subject to fading from exposure to heat and light.

entirely transparent. Illuminated by transmitted monochromatic light, however, and viewed from the proper angle, it will display an image.

Today's hologram cannot be projected on a screen, but it *can* be viewed with the naked eye, and thus also with an electronic eye (television camera). The playback device scans the image with a laser beam and displays it, as in the case of EVR, on a television screen.

At the present time, RCA has demonstrated in the laboratory a method of recording video images on a very thin transparent vinyl tape, about the size of 16mm film and no more expensive than paper. As in the case of EVR, original production must be done in film, live TV, or video tape. If the original is video, it must be converted to film, much as with EVR, using an electron beam recording (EBR) process. The film is then converted, by means of a laser, into a hologram film, from which multiple hologram prints may be made. The hologram film is made in the conventional manner of making holograms. A laser light is divided into two beams; one passes through the film as though the film were being projected; the other, the reference beam, follows an unobstructed route of equal length. They arrive together at a film which is coated with a special emulsion. Since one beam has passed through an image, the two are not identical, and interference patterns are created between them. The film emulsion is partially softened by the laser light; development washes away the softened material, leaving a mechanical pattern of hills and valleys. The film is then electroplated with nickel; which, when it is stripped away, retains a cast of the pattern. This nickel film is then used as a master for embossing the hologram pattern on other material. Thin vinyl film is run in contact with the nickel master between heated rollers, and the hologram pattern is embossed upon it. Large quantities of very inexpensive prints may be made in this manner. Holographic recording is unique in that practically no amount of dirt, scratches or other surface blemishes will have any noticeable effect on picture quality.

For the user, there will be little apparent difference between holographic recording and EVR. Programs for each will come in a cartridge which is inserted into a machine and viewed on a television screen.

Internally, the RCA "SelectaVision" device will consist of a simple helium-neon laser, the film transport system, and a vidicon camera. The laser illuminates the entire film frame, and reconstructs the image. It is viewed by a vidicon camera from an angle which is off the axis of the laser beam, the conventional method of viewing holograms. The image on the vidicon tube is then scanned in the normal manner and transmitted as a video signal for display on a TV screen.

At this writing RCA expects to have a color system with sound available for the home market within two years. While the final form of the home player has not yet been determined, it is expected to be no longer than a small suitcase, so as to rest on the top of a home television set. Cartridges on the order of six inches in longest dimension and about three quarters of an inch thick will carry a half-hour of program; or, if they are made dual-track, an hour.

As with EVR, this process is suitable only for central production on a multiple-print, wide-distribution basis. RCA itself will probably provide the only laboratory service for SelectaVision, just as CBS will for EVR, at least at the start. Given sufficient volume (at least 200 prints of a given subject) both EVR and holographic recording promise to be very much less expensive than conventional film or video tape processes.

### Video Tape

When video tape first became available, in 1956, it started a revolution in the television industry which was very far-reaching in its effects. Television had been primarily a full telemedium which produced its own software, even though films had always been an important ingredient of television programming and the broadcast of kinerecordings had been increasing. With video tape, there seemed little advantage in doing much live programming anymore. Television changed rapidly from a telecommunication medium to a *transmission* medium: The chief recording medium transmitted continued to be sound film, but video tape soon became a close second.

As we have already noted, video tape provided a recording method which, at least to the average viewer, was entirely indistinguishable from live transmission. It was, in that respect at least, the ideal recording medium. Moreover, video tape could be erased and reused up to 100 times. For purposes of delayed broadcast and short-term storage, video tape was more effective and far less expensive than film television recording, and it quickly replaced most applications of this earlier medium.

Video tape also allowed television-studio schedules to be divorced from transmission schedules. No longer was it necessary, for example, for the cast and crew of a live television drama scheduled for a 12:00 noon broadcast to assemble for rehearsal at 2:00 a.m. Production could be done at any time, as far ahead of the broadcast date as desirable; and it could be done in segments. When a program segment had been recorded, played back and accepted, the sets could be struck and studio areas freed; cast members who had no further appearances could be released; and the length of the role which any crew member had to learn at any one time was greatly reduced.

Live television productions had always been rehearsed and broadcast in very much shorter times than shooting and editing of sound films. (The difference was between 5 and 10 to 1.) This led some producers to experiment with video tape as a means of producing films, for television distribution at least, and later for theaters.*

One discouraging result of the attempts to short-cut the time and cost of film-making by using television-studio techniques was that without the pressure of imminent air time, both cast and crew worked more slowly. Since errors in the final performance were no

---

*In 1964, Warner Brothers released a motion-picture version of "Hamlet," and in 1965 Magna produced "Harlow," both of which were theatrical releases produced originally on video tape.

longer irretrievable and scenes could be reshot, there were many more errors, and much reshooting was needed. Creative directors and producers, never really satisfied with the results of slap-dash television production, were suddenly able to reshoot scenes which they considered unsatisfactory—and therefore did so. The rate of retaking and overshooting began to approach that in standard film production (between 3 and 10 retakes per scene).

As a result of producing in takes and in short sequences instead of all in a piece, the editing process became more and more complex. Editing had been totally lacking from the production schedule in live television because all editing was perforce done at the time of shooting. In video tape production, the time and cost of editing soon began to approach that of film production. Video tape costs did not ever become as great as film costs, however, and many regular television programs are produced today on tape rather than film, primarily for economic reasons.

In instructional television, where the technical costs of equipment and recording stock are proportionately larger budget items than they are in entertainment production, video tape provides a more feasible medium than film for many purposes. This has been increasingly true with the development of inexpensive, portable video tape recorders. At the present writing, there are about 40 manufacturers of portable video tape equipment. From the 1956 cost of $75,000 for the first VTR machines that appeared on the market, the cost of equipment providing comparable picture quality dropped to around $25,000, and equipment designed to somewhat lower quality standards went down to $12,000, then $8,000, then $3,000. In the middle sixties, VTR machines costing under $1,000 appeared in department stores for sale to the home market. The outlook is that the cost of such machines may eventually be reduced to under $500. Standard broadcast machines use 2-inch tape; the less expensive models generally use 1-inch, 3/4-inch or 1/2-inch tape. Two Japanese firms introduced 1/2-inch and 3/4-inch video tape in cassette form during 1969. Since video recorders are only slightly more complicated to operate than audio recorders, and the tape is similarly reusable, video tape now ranks with audio tape as a leading home- or local-production medium.

The most common use of portable video tape equipment is as a learner aid; that is, a device which a learner uses in practicing the performance of a skill, with or without the presence of a teacher. The learner interacts, essentially, with the device. Thus, portable video tape is frequently used for individual or group self-confrontation or self-observation. A student diver performs and then observes his performance critically; group members interact in a discussion situation, then view themselves and objectively discuss their techniques of interaction. In teacher-training, the procedure of teaching a short segment and then observing oneself critically is being called "micro-teaching." But these are not examples of video tape used as a communication medium. It is probably safe to say that the main application of portable VTR in communication today is in the recording of lectures, conferences, interviews, and the like, for reference or for later playback to persons who were not able to be present at the actual events. There is increasing use of these machines, however, in the production of instructional materials.

The only standards today in the field of video tape are those that apply to broadcast equipment, where all makes and models of machines will play any tape made on any other machine that adheres to the same broadcast standard.* Broadcast standard equipment is expensive ($25,000 to $100,000 per unit), and 2-inch tape stock costs about $200 an hour. Few closed-circuit users can afford it.

A few portable VTR models are capable of playing back video tapes with the Electronic Industries Association's (EIA) synchronizing pulses** which are legally required if the tapes are

---

*All broadcast standard recorders use 2-inch tape and contain four video heads which scan transversely. Some run at 7-1/2 inches per second, however, and some at 15; some record only color, some only black and white; some are "high-band," and some "low-band."

**A standard established by the Electronic Industries Association to assure compatibility.

to be broadcast. All manufacturers claim interchangeability of tapes between individual machines of the same model, although this is not always fully satisfactory. Few manufacturers can exchange tapes between different models within their own line; none can exchange tapes with any of the other manufacturers' models. (Each make and model uses a different combination of tape size, speed, number of heads, and various other factors.) If one or two manufacturers' models capture the greater part of the market, other firms will begin to introduce machines that can interchange tapes with this majority, and standards will thus be set. Until this takes place, however, the central distribution of tapes to users with many kinds of machines will be done by rerecording from one type of tape to another. Rerecording of prints from a master must be done in any case for large-scale distribution, but the necessity for a recording service to have so many types of recorders on hand makes the service more expensive and less satisfactory than it will be after standardization.

## CLASS II: AUDIO-STILL-VISUAL MEDIA

Audio-still-visual media are capable of all the representations of information that Class I media can provide, except that they cannot represent visual images in motion. However, they have the advantages of being very much less expensive and of having simpler hardware, simpler production procedures and simpler transmission problems. A single television channel, for example, may transmit, by a proposed process known as time sharing, a different set of still pictures at the rate of one picture every ten seconds to each of at least 300 separate viewers. Ten seconds of sound film, to give another example, can contain 240 separate still images; thus, if used for still images, the same film-stock material can hold up to 240 times as much information.

### Still-Picture Television
Still-picture television is the most promising unexplored

telecommunication medium. It appears to approach both television's universality of use and radio's inexpensiveness. Still pictures and sound may be broadcast in two ways, which are sufficiently different to justify classing the two as distinct media: slow-scan and time-shared television. Because slow-scan TV has seen only experimental use, and time-shared TV has merely been proposed, they can be discussed only in terms of their inherent characteristics. How they could be applied is only speculation, but the indications are strong that they can be used for many instructional purposes. It is easy to see how still-TV-by-wire might be an improvement over the more cumbersome telelecture system, or broadcast-still-TV could do more easily what radiovision is doing now, albeit at a higher cost. In a world where the usable electromagnetic spectrum is less and less able to accommodate all of the broadcasting demands on it, a system that can fit up to 300 still-TV channels into the space of one standard television channel may be very practical indeed, even if the lack of motion somewhat lowers its effectiveness. Some of the digital methods of encoding and transmitting still pictures developed for the space program may soon be applied, and this could make the medium even more efficient in its use of the broadcast spectrum.

*Slow-Scan TV.* If a picture is scanned at a slow enough rate, it can be transmitted over a standard telephone line or broadcast on a radio channel. Facsimile does this also, but over a period of minutes instead of seconds; facsimile produces a hard-copy printout, while slow-scan TV is generally conceived as a system which merely displays a still picture on a CRT screen.

The first such system used a display tube with a long persistence phosphor on which the image could be slowly built up and retained until the next image was needed. The more time devoted to its transmission, the higher the definition of the picture could be. The drawback of this system, however, making it unsuitable for instruction, was that the viewer was required to spend the 10- to 40-second period prior to each display watching as the picture slowly built up, line by line, on an initially dark screen.

A second display technique removes the first picture line by line as the second is laid down, thus creating the effect of a wipe moving from left to right across the screen. This is no more suitable for instructional purposes, however, than the first method; both risk distracting the student by the action of image build-up, which, if pictures are to change every 10 seconds, would be a constant process. A means must be devised for storing a picture at the receiving end until it is complete, then displaying it with an instantaneous cut from the preceding picture. Also, if standard television systems are to be used for the display, which is the most practical because such equipment is almost ubiquitous, there must be a means of "replenishing" the television picture every 1/30 second. This is the problem of scan conversion (converting from slow-scan to standard scan rates).

One laboratory solution to this problem has been to incorporate "storage tubes" in the still-TV receiver, on which each successive visual may be built up and held while the preceding visual is being displayed.

Another alternative for short-term storage at the receiving end is the video disc, a system which is already appreciably cheaper than the storage tube, and is expected to become substantially less expensive. A video disc also has the capability of recording hundreds of pictures and, with multiple pick-up heads, can reproduce as many as 64 separate images simultaneously for 64 different users. Currently available storage tubes are capable of storing only one image at a time.

The production problem in sending live programs by slow-scan TV is that while the audio is transmitted and displayed in real time, the video requires a finite period to be transmitted, and a picture cannot appear in its entirety on receiver screens until some seconds after the decision has been made to transmit it. In other words, for proper synchrony, pictures must be sent in advance of the moment they are needed.

The slow-scan TV director will thus operate a little differently from the conventional television director. Using several cameras, he will anticipate what should be shown next, as all television directors do, and if there are several possibilities he may send them all, to be received and stored at all receiving locations. When the moment comes in the program to display a given image, he will punch the appropriate button on his switching system. This action will then send a control pulse (possibly superimposed on the audio program as an inaudible tone) to all receivers, directing them to display the appropriate picture.

Slow-scan equipment was developed by Glen Southworth of Colorado Video and first applied instructionally at Colorado State University during the summer of 1969 to interconnect the Fort Collins and the Sterling, Colorado, campuses for the sharing of formal engineering courses. The University of Wisconsin Extension Department, in association with the Westinghouse Corporation, developed a slow-scan system to interconnect the University of Wisconsin Medical School with several nearby hospitals in the state. Available information on this system indicated that more than one still picture is transmitted in advance of use and stored at receiving locations. There is a possibility that in the future FM radio may be used for the picture transmission. A proposed system, called PictuRadio, would use FM channel sub-carriers, a maximum of four of which can carry audio or video messages without affecting the FM station's primary radio channel.

*Time-Shared Television.* A proposed alternative to slow scan as a method of transmitting still-picture television involves a television transmitter and channel used jointly among a very large number of users. It is estimated that ". . . if the normal TV frame rate were reduced from 30 frames per second to one frame every ten seconds on the average, 300 television sets could receive different individual stationary frames at the 'same' time. If digital data processing procedures replace video techniques, a significant amplification of the 300 factor might be achieved."[9] In other words, since a television transmitter normally sends out 300 individual frames every 10 seconds, each could be different and be selected automatically by a different user. A given program would thus consist of, say, frame 1, frame 301, frame 601, etc., another program of frames 2, 302, 602, and so forth.

Time-shared television would not reach its most economical level, of course, until a channel was fully saturated with 300 users. It is possible, however, that experimentation might start with the use of an existing television channel only at certain hours that would not interfere with its regular operation.

Time-shared television is not even in the laboratory stage; it exists only as a proposed method, the details of which have been sketched out in the TICCET* study by the Mitre Corporation. In theory, each individual user would receive a new picture every 10 seconds, which, according to the TICCET system, would have been selected by a central computer from its tape, disc and core memories. A terminal memory (storage tube or disc) is also required, to store the frame after it has been transmitted and reconstitute it every 1/30 second so it can be displayed on a standard television monitor. Since the original study, TICCET was developed and tested as a single-school system using a small local computer. Prerecorded video disc materials would be hand-carried to the school rather than broadcast. The wired distribution system works on the same time-sharing principle, however.

*Recorded Still-TV.* Still-picture television may be recorded by several media, magnetic tape and disc being the most successful; phonograph records have been used, and, theoretically, such recording media as sound slide and sound filmstrip are applicable if the necessary interface hardware is developed. A single video disc 14 inches in diameter can hold 900 concentric tracks, each of which may contain a still picture of equal quality with pictures from television studio cameras or televised slides. Recording on both sides of a disc gives a total capacity of 1800 still pictures. Video disc, however, is not being considered at present as program-carrying software, since discs cost, today, at least $250 each. Future 6-inch discs, in quantity, will cost much less, along with the hardware required to record and play back. Audio is not now recorded on video discs, but if the material costs come down with time, and certain other problems are solved,

*An acronym for Time-shared Interactive Computer-Controlled Educational Television.

audiovisual discs may someday become a medium for program distribution. There has been some experimentation by a Japanese company with a lightweight, thin, flexible video-recording material called "video sheet," which could possibly be reproduced quite inexpensively in large quantities.

Because phonograph records can be pressed and distributed cheaply in large quantities, at least one firm has developed an audiovisual system using this medium. Under the name Phonovid, this Westinghouse system was demonstrated publicly a few years ago, then disappeared. The playback system required a 16-inch phonograph record with a standard high-quality audio-pickup device. The record turned at a speed sufficient to play a side in 20 minutes. Pictures were scanned line by line at the rate of one every six seconds, for a total of 200 pictures per side. Each picture was fed to one of two storage tubes where it was slowly written on the target of the tube. It was then immediately scanned back into a television display system at the standard rate of once every 1/30 second for six seconds, while the next slow-scan picture was being written onto the target of the other storage tube. The costs of this storage-tube scan-conversion method made Phonovid economically impractical; it has been estimated that the manufacturer would have had to charge $10,000 each for sets of playback equipment. It now appears that video-disc scan-conversion equipment will help solve this problem. The possibility of video and audio recording on phonograph disc is by no means eliminated, therefore, and may still be resurrected in some future system.

A more immediately practicable method appears to be the use of standard audio tape as the recording medium. With sound and picture on the two racks of a stereo tape, either in loop cartridge or on reel-to-reel tape, a system similar to Phonovid but using disc equipment for scan conversion could be developed. Standard video tape may also be used for storing still-picture images, as is done in Videofile. On one reel of video tape normally capable of recording an hour of television, 108,000 still pictures may be recorded. A still may then be transferred to a video-disc buffer (in 1/30 second), from which it may be played over and over as long as needed for a television display.

Pima College, in Tucson, Arizona, has a video disc still-picture and sound system planned. At the start of a study period, for instance, 900 still pictures will be dubbed off video tape onto a master disc. When a user needs a picture, it will be dubbed off the master onto a buffer disc in 1/30 second, thus immediately freeing the master for other users. The picture will then be picked up off the buffer disc every 1/30 second and fed to a standard television display system for as long as it may be required. Buffer discs are two-sided, and they accommodate up to 8 pickup heads per side. Since each user must have his own pickup head, 16 learners may use one buffer disc simultaneously. Pima College plans to have one master and three buffer discs, thus accommodating 48 learner positions with still-picture television display.

A system designed by Earl Morrison at the University of Texas Dental Branch in Houston will use video disc to make still television available on an individual-access basis from some 100 student positions. This will be the first serious use of three-dimensional images in any instructional medium; some hundreds of still-picture stereo pairs will be available to the dental students in their laboratories, as well as some stereo motion video, plus live stereo television from a television instructor, for students who need individual help. Instruction may be programmed in four differently paced tracks or in branching formats. Each student finds the track that is best suited to his individual pace, switching between tracks at will. Each student may access any of the materials that are available, independently of all other students who are using the same system. Each student will have "his own" 1-inch audio and video buffer and "his own" track and pick-up head on a still-video buffer disc. The audio-video buffer will run at 1 inch per second when carrying audio and the pulses to select still images, and 10 inches per second where it is carrying audio and motion video. It is capable of running at 1000 inches per second in fast forward and reverse modes.

*Sound Filmstrip (Slide Film)*

The sound filmstrip, since it presents sound as well as picture, is a more effective medium than filmstrip, especially for persuasion, where the human voice can be very valuable. Sound-filmstrip playback equipment tends to be about twice the cost of silent-system equipment, averaging around $230 per unit instead of $120. Its major use to date has been in sales, where it provides the visiting salesman with a presentation that is considerably cheaper and more portable than a sound motion picture and its equipment, and that lacks only the element of motion. About half of the more than 50 models available in 1968 were equipped with small built-in rear or front projection screens, which are part of the case or which fold out from it. These units are not designed for group viewing, and those with built-in screens could not be so used, since the screens are rarely larger than about 8 x 10 inches.

The sound portion of this medium is, with only one manufacturer's system excepted, recorded on a separate disc or tape, which is synchronized with the filmstrip. It would be more correct to say that the filmstrip is synchronized with the sound, since the sound runs continuously and sets the pace, and the pictures must follow. About half the units on the market require an operator to advance the filmstrip manually, either at the projector or remotely, in response to a "beep" in the sound. The other half, however, have some automatic means whereby a subsonic pulse or a light-reflecting spot triggers the mechanism and advances the filmstrip.

A new type of sound-filmstrip device recently released by CBS Laboratories combines sound and picture into one piece of software—not by putting the sound on the film, but by putting the pictures on the record. Actually, the pictures are photographed onto a flat ring of film, which surrounds a small LP record; then the whole is enclosed in a transparent plastic cartridge, leaving only the playing side of the record exposed. In operation, the record spins within the ring of pictures, which are advanced by an inaudible tone in the recording. The cartridge is 5 inches in diameter and 1/4-inch thick, and it will probably sell for about $3 or $4. The record holds 18 minutes of sound, and there is room for 52 pictures around the edge. A small and highly portable projection device is provided, with a built-in front projection screen on the inside of the cover, which is set in position when the cover is raised. The device is also equipped with four response buttons, so it can be used as a simple teaching machine. It is designed for use only in the individual mode, since the screen is only about 8 x 5-1/2 inches.

This device is not amenable to the local production of software, at least not directly. A service will probably be established that will take a set of slides produced by the client, plus an audio tape to which the slides are to be synchronized, duplicate the images in the ring shape, and rerecord the sound onto the record; the whole will then be sealed into its cartridge and returned to the client.

The sound filmstrip appears to be assuming a much more important role in instruction than it has played in the past. It has been mentioned before that the actual need for motion in cognitive learning is probably very much smaller than has usually been assumed, and still pictures can do as well as motion pictures in the majority of cases. Sound filmstrip may well be the medium with the greatest unused instructional potential.

### Sound Slide-Set

The sound slide-set consists of a set of slides contained generally within the magazine of an automatic projector, the advance of which is controlled by an audio tape which plays on a separate tape-playback device. The sound slide-set was made possible only within the last few years by two developments: (1) the automatic 2 x 2 slide projector* and (2) audio-tape control devices.

*In 1968 there were 15 models of automatic-magazine 2 x 2 slide projectors. Some of these held 80 to 100 slides per magazine.

Automatic slide projectors are intended, usually, to be used in situations requiring remote control. The lecturer carries a pushbutton device in his hand, or one is attached to his podium; he then advances his slides at will. The electrical system for activating slide advance, however, may take its impulses from any source, and cues on an audio tape may replace the manual pushbutton. Generally, the tape-playback device is equipped with a sensor consisting of two contacts which ride against the tape. The space between these two terminations is the only open segment of a circuit which, when energized, can activate the slide-advance mechanism. A small pressure-sensitive segment of metal tape is attached to the audio tape; when this reaches the two contacts it completes the circuit momentarily and advances the slide.

Other systems use a two-track tape-playback device, one track being used to carry the program sound, the other to carry audio pulses which advance the projector.

Sound slide-set is not a medium that lends itself to mass distribution. Slides would have to be distributed in relatively bulky and expensive magazines; and there would always be the hazard of people opening the magazines to use single slides, and damaging slides or mixing up the sequence. Furthermore, there is no standardization of tape-playback cuing systems; few individuals or institutions have any such equipment at all. Consequently, this medium is, at least at present, appropriate only for local production and use. An instructor or a department, for instance, might provide recorded presentations which could be administered either in the group or the individual mode.

Sound slide-set is one of six media and multimedia combinations which involve separate sound. Three of these are telemedia (telelecture, telewritevision and radiovision), and three are recording media (sound filmstrip, sound slide-set and separate-sound film).* The sound portion of the three telemedia is a live,

---

*Separate-sound film is discussed under Sound Films; the tele-multimedia combinations will be described later in this section.

simultaneous, real-time transmission, while the visual portions are distributed by mail ahead of time. Visuals are changed manually in response to audible cues in the sound program. In the recording media, the sound and picture portions, although separate, are always kept together; they are often filed in the same box. Slide advance, in these media, can be automated. Thus, they are not as dependent on the human factor as the separate-sound telemedia are for (1) matching the correct sound to the correct set of visuals, and (2) proper manual slide advancement. In addition, they do not depend on the reliability of transportation, which in some localities today is highly questionable. However, if transport of a recording medium is delayed, the whole lesson is merely delayed; but if the visual portion of a radiovision lesson is delayed, the lesson is lost, since the broadcast sound portion must proceed on schedule.

### Sound-on-Slide

Sound-on-slide systems enclose 2 x 2-inch slides in larger holders or cartridges that carry an area of magnetic material for recording. In the 3M model this is a circular area surrounding the slide. While the slide is projected, an audio head rotates around it following a spiral track. It can either record or play back up to 35 seconds of sound. A magazine holds 36 slides. The Kalart model provides a combination cartridge which holds, in addition to the slide, 60 seconds of tape in a small cassette. A circular magazine holding 40 cartridges is placed on an Eastman Carousel or Ektographic slide projector in place of the usual slide tray.

Sound-on-slide is a highly flexible medium. Slides may be rearranged within a magazine; sound for a given slide may be changed while the slide is kept, or the slide changed without touching the sound. Narration may be recorded and rerecorded until it is satisfactory. Once on the slide, the sound is locked in and must remain in synchrony until the slide is removed from the holder.

The present cost of sound-on-slide is, of course, much greater than that of sound filmstrip, and therefore it cannot compete with

other systems in large-market distribution of multiple-print software. It is primarily a medium for local production of one-of-a-
kind slide sets.


### Sound Page

There is a machine on the market today, called Studymaster,
which is essentially a printed page with magnetic sound. Sound is
recorded in a spiral track on the back side of a printed sheet, 8-1/2
by 11-3/4 inches in size. This medium is usable only in the
individual mode, but is capable of carrying sound, picture and
print, and the visual elements may, of course, be reproduced in
color if desired.

The learner uses a small table-top playback device, about the
same dimensions as the printed sheet and three or four inches
thick. He places the sound page on the machine, dons earphones,
and starts the playback. The sheet does not revolve, but stays
readable while the playback head revolves beneath it, moving
toward the center of the circle as it goes. This is not to be
confused with the plastic phonograph record; the face of such a
record may contain visual elements, but these cannot be seen
*while* the audio is playing, since the disc must revolve.


### Talking Book

In this audio-still-visual medium, an ordinary bound and
printed book is used, on the pages of which horizontal strips of
magnetic oxide are printed. Speech is recorded on these strips to
correspond to the adjacent print or picture which the page
contains. When used in the learning of reading, for example, or a
foreign language, a small reader is placed on the strip; it runs
across the page picking up the audio and feeding it into a set of
headphones, while the learner simultaneously reads the words or
follows the pictures.[10]

## CLASS III: AUDIO-SEMIMOTION MEDIA

### Telewriting

The telewriting medium transmits two components: the voice of an instructor and his handwriting. Handwriting can, of course, include printing and drawing. Telewriting involves a type of motion or animation: the build-up of written characters or the gradual appearance of parts of a diagram as it is drawn. This feature can be of value when gradual appearance is desired—the instructor may use the device much as he would use a chalkboard. As with the chalkboard, however, there is a basic limitation which prevents an entire visual from being presented at once (unless a chalkboard is used as a more permanent display).

The method of transmitting writing by wire was invented almost as long ago as the telephone. It was originally called the Telautograph (now used as the company name of one firm which manufactures telewriting equipment). Although both horizontal and vertical components of the writing movement must be transmitted, transmission requires about 1/4 the bandwidth of a standard telephone channel. The total cost for both sound and writing is generally about that of two telephone lines. For many years telewriting existed as a means of individual communication, employed generally in industry, where it was desirable to communicate written orders quickly. Telewriting assured that the message went immediately and that it remained in a permanent form. The message appeared on a roll of paper in its original size, so this was essentially an individual communication medium.

In recent years, equipment has been devised which projects the telewritten image onto a screen, and telewriting has become a group instructional medium. Some telewriting display devices use the opaque-projection principle, reflecting light from the surface of the paper, then projecting this with an overhead lens and mirror in the fashion of a standard overhead transparency projector. Other devices replace the opaque paper with a roll of clear acetate, and shine the light through it, putting considerably more lumens on the screen. Devices of this type are suitable for auditorium projection.

Telewriting has been used as a substitute for instructional television. It appears to be most satisfactory in teaching courses where the visual element generally consists mainly of chalkboard writing, such as in mathematics and engineering. When distances are great between schools, telewriting can be economically feasible, where television is not. It is therefore being used in many areas countywide to share the instructor resources of a number of high schools in the presentation of subjects such as physics, for which good teachers are rare. One current project of this type ties together schools throughout the state of Wyoming and parts of northern Colorado.

### Telewritevision

Telewritevision is a name the author has given to a multimedia variation of the telewriting medium in which local visual materials are involved, making it possible to include still pictures and nearly all other types of graphic materials, in color if desired, along with the transmitted elements of sound and writing and/or drawing. Telewritevision provides more ways of representing information than are possible with telewriting, and thus is to telewriting as radiovision is to radio.

Telewritevision is most successful when the transparency projection method of display is used, and both the transmitted telewriting and the local visual materials are displayed by the same projector. A special frame is provided in some telewriting projectors into which transparent visuals may be placed and then changed by sliding them in and out. It is possible to slide a map, for example, into both the lecturer's transmitting device and the receiver device, so the lecturer may actually draw, write on, or point to the surface of the map, locating points and areas. When a drawing is completed, the lecturer touches a particular area with his stylus, and the rolls of acetate on his and on all receiving devices advance to another clear area without affecting the visual over which the acetate is superimposed.

Sylvania's "Blackboard by Wire" system is similar to what has been described except that display is effected via closed-circuit television monitors. A school that has a television installation will need to add a conversion device. This consists of a storage tube to display the image until it is erased by the sender, and a small TV camera to pick up this image and feed it into the closed-circuit system. Unlike the optical projection method, only the writing appears; the shadow of the writing stylus and its harness is not visible. However, somewhat larger than normal handwriting is necessary.

### Recorded Telewriting

Telewriting may be recorded on dual-track stereo audio tape, the audio on one track and the two dimensions of stylus movement on the other. Live telewriting is generally preferred, however, because of the possibility of audio feedback; since telephone line rates are based on two-way lines, the feedback line is available anyhow.

### Audio Pointer

A new medium made its appearance just as this book was going to press, utilizing the semimotion effect of *pointing* rather than *build-up* as telewriting does. Called Audi/Pointer, this currently available device combines an ordinary audio tape cassette with a set of large paper charts or diagrams.

A chart some 12 by 8 inches in size is placed in proper register on a display device like a large microfilm reader. An audio cassette is inserted in the machine; the user listens to narration through earphones. At the same time a second track on the same tape controls the movement of a spot of light which strikes the paper from the back side pointing out appropriate places in the illustration, tracing paths of flow or directions of movement.

## CLASS IV: MOTION-VISUAL MEDIA

### Silent film

Before the invention of the sound film, in the late 1920's, the silent film had known 30 years as a mass medium of tremendous popularity. Narration and dialogue were supplied by titles separate from the action and spliced in. A few creative filmmakers managed to devise film action that was self-explanatory and could do without titles; generally, titles were considered a necessary evil and were kept as short as possible. After the sound film had taken over the theaters in a communications revolution, silent film remained for another 15 years or so a medium for nontheatrical films, educational films and, predominantly in the 8mm size, home movies. After World War II, sound film became the preferred medium in the nontheatrical field, but did not effectively reach the home market until the development of 8mm sound in the late 1960's. At present, silent film is still the predominant medium for home movies and, save audio tape, is used more than any other medium for local or home recording. While there is some central distribution of silent films for screening on home projectors, almost all the silent film used in the home is homemade. It should be remembered, however, that in this application film is more a communication aid than a medium, since amateur moviemakers generally project their own films and contribute the necessary verbal narration at the time.

In the mid-1960's a movement began among educational innovators to develop and encourage the use of 8mm film in instruction. Equipment became available which, for the first time, would project films enclosed in a plastic cartridge. This is a relatively small cartridge, about 5 inches in diameter, holding a maximum of only 4-1/2 minutes of film. Since the film is in an endless loop, the end spliced to the beginning, there is no rewinding; the film simply must be run through to completion before it can be started again. Because of these advantages and limitations, a new variety of instructional film has appeared—the single-concept film, used to present only one idea, develop it, and end. It is used as a resource for lesson presentation in the group mode, or more often, for review and study in the individual mode. A recent directory lists some 6,000 single-concept silent-film loops in 4-minute cartridges. It is possible to film "home movies" and have them returned in a cartridge if desired. The medium does not lend itself to the editing and splicing of individual shots, however, since a loop cartridge will not run well when the film contains splices. Loading of the cartridge is too complex for the amateur, and is generally provided as a laboratory service.

Standards for silent film have varied considerably over the nearly 70 years of its history, the difference between one standard and another being based mainly on film width. Throughout its history, silent film has run at a standard speed of 16 frames per second, which is two-thirds the speed of sound film. (Sound film has to run faster because of the need of a higher speed for quality sound.) The first standard was 35mm, which is still used in theaters without wide screens. The 16mm standard was established in the 1920's, and in 1935 standard 8mm film was established. Experiments were made with 4mm film, but they were abandoned because the image quality was unsatisfactory. Now that finer-grained film stock is available, 4mm film is being discussed again. A European standard was also set in the mid-1930's: 9-1/2mm, with the sprocket holes in the center of the film between frames.

In the midst of the development of 8mm film cartridges and the sudden increase in the use of 8mm film in instruction, including the emergence of the single-concept film, 8mm film itself went through a major revolution. A new film standard, Super 8, made its appearance. Although the film is the same width as standard 8mm, the image size is about 50 percent greater, due to the use of smaller sprocket holes and slightly fewer frames per foot. Picture quality is so clearly improved that there is little doubt that Super 8 will rapidly replace standard 8mm film in both instruction and home movies. Many single-concept films are now available in both sizes; others are available only in standard 8mm, and some of the newer productions are being released only in Super 8.

## CLASS V:  STILL-VISUAL MEDIA

Class V contains the media that represent information in pictorial or symbolic form without motion. This class includes the medium of print, the most widely useful of all communication media. Its success is due mainly to the fact that it is a most practical form of reproduction of materials for use in the individual mode. Another still-visual medium, the silent filmstrip, is also widely used. A third medium of this class, termed "picture set," includes all kinds of picture sets (with captions, labels, etc.) which are not contained in a fixed order on a strip of film or bound together in pages. Finally, there are microform and video file, which are basically information media used at present primarily for storage and retrieval purposes.

An interesting and important characteristic of still-visual media is that their programs are not locked into the dimension of time. In that respect, they do not seem like programs in the usual sense—they do not "run." Program presentations in any of the other media classes generally proceed forward from start to finish once they are begun, especially if they are being presented in the group mode. Only with media that can be presented in the individual mode is the receiver free of this constraint, and then only if he has playback apparatus which at least gives him stop-start control. Audio and video tape media, with their fast-forward and fast-reverse modes, are beginning to have the capability of internal random access (access within a program as opposed to *external* random access, which applies to the selection of programs). Audio-disc and video-disc devices give the user a faster internal random access than any other means. The nonlinear presentation of still pictures and print, tied neither to the one-word-after-another stream of audio narration nor to the filmic stream of the motion picture, allows the user to set his own pace, skip, review, or even start at the end and work forward if that is what he likes to do.

Many of the devices in the filmstrip medium do not actually allow random access within the program (to reach frame ten from frame five, the user must momentarily display the intermediate frames). However, other filmstrip and slide projection devices do allow one to go directly from five to ten without displaying the frames between, and all filmstrip devices will, of course, allow the user to proceed at his or his group's own pace.

### Facsimile

Facsimile is the only telemedium in the still-visual class. Since still-visual media are not time-based, telecommunication has a different value here than it does for any of the other media classes. Facsimile is a means of transmitting still-visual materials, in which the message is not perceived by the user in real time. In other words, no one expects to sit in front of a facsimile receiver and absorb the program as it comes in. Facsimile would be a poor medium for two-way interaction between sender and receiver.

Facsimile is essentially a transmission system, rather than a communication medium, at least as it is presently employed. Nothing except recorded materials can enter a facsimile system; nothing except recorded materials can be put out. Facsimile is also a relatively slow means of transmission relative to other telemedia. A page of information requires from approximately six seconds to six minutes to transmit.

Currently, facsimile finds its greatest usefulness in the transmission of pictorial and line-graphic materials. Data in alphanumeric form can be more quickly and inexpensively transmitted by teletype. Facsimile is used to transmit engineering drawings, weather maps and similar materials under conditions where mail transportation would be too slow. Local television stations receive news photos by facsimile from central news agencies. Input equipment for facsimile systems is available to take still-visual materials in any of the recording-media forms, in nearly any size, length, or thickness—even microfilm. Transmission at slow rates may take place over standard direct-dial telephone lines, in conjunction with Dataphone or an acoustic coupler. For faster rates of transmission, special, somewhat broader-band telephone lines are required.

Facsimile signals may be recorded on audio tape running at about five inches per second, which allows for about 80 minutes of recording on a seven inch reel (up to 80 pages). Obviously, recorded facsimile is not an efficient means of information storage, in comparison with microfilm, for example. Its value is as a means of delayed transmission of a message and/or delayed printout at the receiving end.

Facsimile is strictly an information transmission system in its present form. It is possible that with the development of less-expensive equipment, however, facsimile may be integrated with other communication media in multimedia instructional systems to transmit supporting printed materials or, operating in the other direction, to collect student responses, papers, or exams.

RCA's proposed "Edufax" system makes possible the transmission of facsimile signals on an operating television station without affecting the regular television signal.[11] This is accomplished through the utilization of intermittent unused time when no signal is normally being transmitted, i.e., during the vertical blanking interval between TV fields. Edufax signals can thus be received wherever the TV signal is received, and extra costs for the transmission function alone are zero. Encoding and decoding equipment is of course required.

Five lines of the standard 525 TV scanning lines are used; in the receiver these are displayed on an internal screen across which electrostatic paper (similar to that used in photocopying machines) is drawn. One page of 5 by 6-1/2 inches (about 1/3 standard page area) is presently turned out every 10 seconds. This probably allows for a line 40 legible characters in length, about what a standard television system can display.

## The Printed Page

Since the nature of the print medium in all its subclasses is well known, it will not be necessary to go into any detailed description here. Recent developments, such as the techniques of photocomposition, promise to bring the costs of high-quality printing and high-definition pictorial reproduction down into the current cost range of second-class methods. These improvements may stimulate increased use of print media, as did the earlier development of the inexpensive paperback book.

The printed page is the most useful communication medium today; it is by far the most heavily used; and it has such great inherent advantages that it will probably remain the most useful medium for some time to come. Nevertheless, it remains a communication medium, and has many of the same advantages and disadvantages as other media, when compared with conventional face-to-face communication. Print is impersonal, canned and standardized—all receivers read exactly the same words in their separate copies of the same book. If a reader does not understand, he cannot ask the author a question. Champions of the traditional in education frequently point out these factors in regard to the newer instructional media, forgetting that they apply equally to the medium of print.

Print, like other media, also has great advantages over face-to-face instruction. Through print, a learner anywhere may study under the finest instructors of the age, or of any age. Conversely, the printed knowledge and wisdom of the greatest teachers may be reproduced in countless duplications and made available to all who wish to know. A man's words thus recorded may be read over and over again, studied, consulted and quoted in still other publications.

But there are now almost a dozen other, newer recording media that can do most of these same things. What advantages has print that will prevent its being superseded by these newer devices? And what disadvantages does it have in relation to the others?

The greatest disadvantage of the print medium is that it requires literacy. In the last 200 years or so, print has become so essential to the conduct of industrial civilization that all of the developed countries have made literacy almost a mandatory qualification for citizenship. This is not true of the undeveloped countries, of course, which include the great majority of the world's people. More than half of the people in the world cannot use the printed page, except in purely pictorial form, some because they are not old enough, the rest because they have not had the educational opportunity of learning to read.

The print medium, of course, presents pictorial representations as well as symbols, so published materials can be of some use to the illiterate. However, this use tends to be in the nature of an instructional aid for a face-to-face verbal explanation, rather than as a self-contained instructional medium. In addition to raising the literacy level, the developing countries will also have to stimulate a steady flow of informational and entertainment materials, newspapers, books in the native language, and the like, lest, as has already happened in some African countries, literacy once attained disappears through disuse. In the meantime, the media that depend on the spoken word for verbal exposition will have a big advantage over print in the undeveloped nations of the world.

The print medium has several advantages over other media. To begin with, print requires no elaborate playback or receiving apparatus for program display. All the expensive equipment of the medium is located in the central point of production and distribution, where the expense is justified by great economies of scale. The extension of the reading public requires no fixed per-reader expenditure except as advertising and promotion may be necessary to motivate new readers, and additional software distribution costs are incurred.

Print is almost the only medium in which the software costs are low enough that individuals may maintain extensive libraries of materials. The closest other media are audio disc and audio tape. A single college student may personally own more hours of instruction in the print medium than his entire university can provide in materials for the sound-film medium, or video tape, for example.

Print gives the learner the maximum freedom of any medium in choosing his modes of access; he can skip, reread, glance ahead and check back. Because of this factor, print is generally the preferred medium for the presentation of material that is difficult for the learner to grasp readily and requires study, thinking and rereading. But whether the material is difficult or easy, print is still the medium with the highest random accessibility *within* the program.

Assuming the existence of a practical index, the system of numbering pages makes finding what you want within a book a fairly easy task. The external problem—finding the book you need by consulting card catalogs or bibliographical files, for instance—may be a great deal more difficult. However, this problem can exist with any medium—we have simply not had to face it in any but the print medium. The information explosion of today is reflected in a print and paper explosion. No one yet seems to be inundated with piles of films or tapes which he has to find time to play. Libraries are still almost exclusively concerned with the print medium, although the trend may be to other media. (As an indication of this trend, in a recent issue of the *Library Journal,* 40 percent of the advertisements concerned materials or equipment for media other than print.)

### Filmstrip

The filmstrip medium consists generally of a recording of still pictures and print on 35mm sprocketed film. Filmstrip systems have also used 16mm film. The recording apparatus is usually standard photographic equipment—often a motion-picture camera adapted to photograph single frames. Filmstrips are played back by a small projector into which the roll of film, generally about three feet long, may be threaded. Frame advance is usually done manually by an operator at the projector or by pushbutton remote control. Some systems encase the filmstrip in a supply-reel cartridge, from which it unwinds and into which it is again rewound after projection. Other systems include a take-up chamber in the cartridge so the filmstrip never leaves the cartridge at all. This is analogous to reel-to-reel tape cassettes, except that reels are not required for filmstrip—the film simply rolls up in a chamber. Continuous-loop filmstrip systems are also in use.

Most filmstrips are produced and projected in color. The most common type, single-frame, carries one picture below the other, like motion-picture film. A less common type, double frame, exposes the film horizontally, in the manner of minicameras, so that each frame lies to the side of the next. Because one double frame utilizes about twice the film area of a single frame, the definition is very much better.

There are four main subclasses of the filmstrip medium, with different software characteristics, each requiring different viewing equipment: 35mm single frame, 35mm double frame, 16mm single frame and 16mm double frame.

Filmstrip has traditionally been a group presentation medium, for use in schools and other non-theatrical situations, as an inexpensive substitute for motion-picture film. It has rarely been preferred over film except for reasons of cost. Like the film medium, it is primarily based on central production and widespread distribution; filmstrips are rarely produced by an individual teacher for his own use.

Combination slide/filmstrip projectors were, in 1961, the most common schoolroom projectors of any type, motion picture or still. At that time it was estimated that there was an average of one filmstrip or slide/filmstrip projector for every eight publicschool classrooms nationwide.[12] The same study estimated that the schools were storing an average of 40 different filmstrips per projector for local use. There were about 14 times as many school-owned filmstrips as school-owned sound films. Except for print, no other medium even approached the filmstrip in number of recordings stored in schools; disc recordings came the closest, with less than half the total number of units. It should be noted that the study did not make a distinction between the silent and sound filmstrip; the sound filmstrips with their associated disc recordings probably accounted for less than 10 percent of the total. Later data indicate that sound filmstrips are growing in popularity while silent filmstrips are declining. Both appear to be losing ground to the sound slide-set and the use of Super 8mm film.

*Picture Set*

A set of pictures may contain both picture and print, and therefore may carry a message that is complete and self-contained. However, its material is not recorded on a single piece of software such as a strip of film. The slide-set, for example, may reach the user safely encased in a magazine for an automatic projector, or as a loose set of slides held together with a rubber band.

Another example is the set of large-size flat pictures reproduced in quantity by photographic enlargement or some graphic process, such as silk-screening or lithography. Such picture sets are distinguished from printed pictures in that they are not screened and produced on a printing press, and hence they are not reproduced in as great a quantity; also, they are generally intended for group use, while pictures on the printed page are usually intended for use in the individual mode.

In some rare instances in information communication, more commonly in artistic expression, pictures will be used to convey a message without the help of words. When, more commonly, picture sets are accompanied by captions, it is generally for use in the individual mode. Pictures without captions are almost always intended to be used in the group mode as instructional aids.

*Microform*

The microform medium is a system of information storage and retrieval designed as a more practical alternative to printed, written, or pictorial materials that exist primarily on paper. Transparent film is generally used for microforms, the two most common types of which are microfilm and microfiche. Microfilm is generally a strip of film 35mm or 16mm wide onto which a large number of individual documents have been photographed. The strip of microfilm is usually contained on a reel or in a cartridge. Unlike filmstrip images in which the height of the frame is 3/4 or less the width, microform images generally reflect the shape of a typical 8-1/2 x 11-inch page, in which the horizontal dimension is the smaller, being only about 3/4 the vertical.

Microfiche is a method of recording in which the images of

individual pages are photographed in rows and columns on a piece of film called a film card or a chip. There are at least six standards that use a microfilm card 4 x 6 inches in size, and at least five formats that use cards of the electronic data processing (EDP) standard size (3-1/4 x 7-3/8 inches). In the 105mm film standard, one very large engineering drawing will occupy the entire area of an EDP card; in the case of HR (High Resolution) Fiche, each card can hold 3200 pages; 4 x 6-inch fiche can carry up to 5600 pages. Maximum reduction ratios for these extremes vary from 12:1 to 150:1. Any reduction ratio higher than 40:1 has come to be called ultramicroform.

A familiar microfiche standard in the EDP card size is the aperture card. In this form, an actual punched card is used, for purposes of machine sorting, which has a window near one end into which an image on 35mm film is inserted. The usual aperture card places only one image in this area, generally an engineering drawing reduced 30:1. The "packed aperture card" puts eight images (8-1/2 x 11-inch documents reduced 24:1) into this space.

Microforms may be read with various types of direct magnifying systems called *viewers,* but they are most commonly projected on individual-viewing projection-screen *readers* which are manually operated.

The primary advantage of microfilming is the saving it affords in storage space and filing equipment. One system, for example, condenses the information that would normally require 100 four-drawer filing cabinets into the space of a single desk top. The ratio of space reduction is sometimes considered to be as high as 500:1. The *Encyclopaedia Britannica* has recently announced a program to develop a series of "Resource and Research Libraries" in ultramicrofiche, intended for new institutions and small colleges. An ultramicroform library of 20,000 volumes will fit on the top of a card table.

The second most important advantage of microform is that access time is greatly reduced. Microfiche, especially, may be filed and accessed very quickly by machine. Finally, mailing facilities and costs are greatly reduced through the use of microforms.

Where large numbers of documents are handled constantly, microform readers can be conveniently located, and personnel can be habituated to their use. Since machine indexing and retrieval systems cannot be located in individual offices, many information users find printed materials in their own personal libraries more convenient, more flexible and easier to access. Some types of work, for example, require that a number of documents be spread out on a desk and consulted in association with each other. A single microform reader could not fill this need.

In recognition of this problem, many manufacturers of microform readers have incorporated hard-copy printout devices into their equipment. This type of hardware is still too expensive for individual office use, however; its most practical application is in libraries and other central information repositories.*

At least one company has incorporated microfiche into a teaching machine, instead of using filmstrip materials. The possibilities of storing a large amount of visual information locally, within the actual display unit, have led to some experimentation with systems that select and control the display of this material by telecommunication from a distant computer. Further development can be expected along this line.

### Video File

The current trend, evident in all the visual media, is toward electronic means of recording, storing, reproducing and/or transmitting information. The electronic approach to information storage and retrieval offers techniques of computer technology to provide shorter indexing and access time, even though the degree of compression of document information may not be as great as ultramicrofiche can make possible.

The Ampex Videofile system, developed in 1964, uses 2-inch video tape as a recording medium; each 8-1/2 x 11-inch document

---

*A recent model, 3M's reader-printer, now sells for about $300. As competitors follow suit, and the trend continues, we may well see the office reader-printer become ubiquitous.

requires about 1/3 inch of tape. A standard 1-hour roll of video tape will thus record some 108,000 images. A display system with four times more detail than a standard home screen is employed, making possible the recording and legible display of 8-1/2 x 11-inch documents containing characters smaller than elite type.

Documents stored on video tape are rerecorded from the master tape onto a buffer disc when requested, then continuously picked off the disc and displayed on high quality television monitors for reading. Hard copy may be obtained if needed via an integral electrostatic printer.

## CLASS VI: AUDIO MEDIA

### Telephone

The telephone has been considered, since its inception, as a private or semiprivate means for conversation at a distance. It can be used, however, as a group instructional medium to bring a lecturer to a distant audience that he could not normally visit in person. The telephone is a more valuable medium than audio recording in such cases, because of the added interest generated by the fact that the presentation is live, and because it is a two-way medium, and members of the audience may engage a speaker in dialogue following his presentation. Instructional uses of the telephone have generally been limited to single groups, although the simultaneous presentation of a verbal lecture to many groups in different locations is readily possible. Two-way dialogue becomes progressively more unwieldy and impractical, however, as the groups become larger.

There have been some interesting applications of the telephone in the individual instructional mode, particularly in the medical field. The medium in these applications is actually audio tape, but the telephone is used as a means of distribution and individual access to a central, possibly distant library of materials. The University of Wisconsin, for example, provides a service of continuing medical education for physicians, using an INWATS* line which a physician can dial into from anywhere in the state toll-free. (The service can be used by anyone in the world if he pays his own toll fee.) The caller receives a short lecture on audio tape, which is played manually by an attendant in response to a verbal request. University of Wisconsin Extension has used two-way telephones in many subject matter areas, for discussion sessions following lecture presentation. Up to 15 responding groups can be accommodated in one such hookup; a number greater than this becomes unwieldy.

### Telelecture

The telelecture is a multimedia system in which the telephone is augmented by the addition of visual elements from locally projected materials. In its simplest form, the visual component may consist of a single projected slide of the face of the lecturer. More commonly, the visual element will consist of a set of slides that have been produced at the institution originating the lecture and sent out in advance to each location where the program will be presented. The sound portion of the program carries cues for the changing of slides, sometimes in the form of beeps, sometimes in the straightforward "next slide, please" style, or, preferably, in requests for slides by number, to assure that they do not become mixed up.

### Radio

Radio, the first of the telecommunication media to make its appearance and still the cheapest to operate in its commonest form, is primarily used as a mass medium. However, it is an individual communication medium in many applications, and it has been heavily used in schools as a medium of group instruction. It is not generally used for instruction in the individual mode, except in central Australia, where elementary and secondary school "classes" are assembled by radio, each pupil sitting alone in

*INWATS (Inward Wide Area Telephone Service).

his isolated sheep-station homestead listening to the teacher and contributing to class discussion via transceiver radio. The effectiveness of this live interconnection is evident in the production of class plays, where pupils in widely separated areas interact dramatically, with perfect timing. So real is this live interconnection that the children often play the productions in actual costume, each player describing his costume to the listening audience before the start of the play.

The usual application of radio to instruction involves the transmission of an audio program which has been previously recorded on tape or disc. Most foreign broadcasting systems devote some of their energies and some of their daytime broadcasting hours to school programs. Radio sets are part of the audiovisual equipment of two-thirds of the school districts in the United States, but are not as widely available as the equipment for the three most used recording media—audio disc, filmstrip and sound film. Although there are now some 3,000 radio stations in this country, instructional broadcasting is largely left to the 450 educational (non-commercial) radio stations. According to a 1966 survey,[13] 85 percent of these educational stations broadcast primarily to the general public, and only about 15 percent program for in-school audiences. The fact that the survey showed there were four record players or tape machines in the nation's schools for each classroom radio receiver reflects the advantages of convenience in the use of recorded materials, especially when these are so inexpensive that individual classroom libraries may be maintained.

Ninety-four percent of the 450 educational radio stations are FM stations; 86 percent are operated by institutions of higher learning. However, most of these licensees participate very little in equipment or programming decisions; they often participate only in budget policy decisions.[14] That educational radio is considered both an inexpensive and an unimportant medium by the organizations that operate stations is shown by the low level of financial support provided. Almost half of all educational radio stations operate on annual budgets of less than $20,000.

An important new development in radio broadcasting, called "SCA"* or "Multiplexing," allows an FM station to carry up to four subcarrier AM channels piggy-back, so to speak, on the main FM carrier, without affecting the regular transmission. Many commercial stations use these extra channels to distribute background music services; some use the extra channels for stereo transmission. To date only about 15 of the educational stations hold authorizations to use multiplexing, but others are making plans to use it. The SCA channels are capable of carrying facsimile, slow-scan television, teletype, or telewriting, and some of these media are being considered today by broadcasters of instructional radio programs.

The SCA channels can be received only by a special multiplex receiver or adapter, which is at present as expensive as a good radio. This need for special receiving equipment puts SCA into a different programming category—it cannot be considered an open-circuit medium. Those broadcasters who service a community with multiplexed background music provide receivers as part of their service, treating SCA as though it were a closed-circuit system.

Even if an inexpensive SCA receiver or adapter is produced for the mass market, it is doubtful whether SCA would rapidly become a mass medium. This, however, may be a blessing; the SCA channels may truly become minority audience services. Even the educational television and radio stations have hesitated to limit their audiences by such programming, and Federal Communications Commission policy has always favored granting licenses for use of the public airwaves to those who proposed to serve the greatest number of the public. Thus, SCA may be of value in professional communications, such as continuing education for doctors, nurses and others in the medical community, and will involve group listening. Special program services for the blind are proposed, along with adult education in many subjects such as agriculture, law and engineering.

*SCA (Subsidiary Communications Authorization).

*Radiovision*

Radiovision is a multimedia system in which the radio medium is augmented through the addition of visual elements at the receiving end. As with the closed-circuit telelecture, these elements are mailed out in advance to the viewing groups. The visual elements consist of slide-sets or filmstrips which may be retained by the schools to which they are sent. This adds an element of permanence to the radio; the visual materials may be used for further study or review.

Radiovision is an important part of the regular broadcast radio service to the French schools. It is also being used in several African countries. It has one great advantage over any other means of audiovisual presentation: it utilizes the very simplest of equipment on the receiving end. A teacher in an African village, for instance, needs only a transistor radio and a kerosene filmstrip projector to have the advantages of the best audio still-visual lesson presentations his country can produce. This is not all of the system, of course. There must be facilities for the production and dissemination of the necessary visual materials, a reliable postal-transportation system, an adequate broadcast signal at the receiving location, a shaded hut for daytime projection, and the teacher must have an accurate watch in order to have his students ready when the program goes on.

Radiovision, like telelecture, requires that the originator of programs make direct correspondence contact with all users. It does not allow for uncontrolled, unknown, hit-or-miss viewership. In this regard, it differs from school radio and television, which is all too often simply pumped out in the hope that a maximum number of classrooms will decide to make use of it. This scattershot approach encourages generalism in the design of programs to make them usable in as many different situations as possible. In a system where each receiving group is known, a much higher degree of specificity is possible.

Several telecommunications media are like radiovision in that they require a direct contact between program originators and viewers or viewing groups—ensuring that the program originators know exactly who their recipients are. These are telelecture, telewriting, telewritevision, telephone and Picturephone. The mass broadcasting media—radio, television and the future still-TV media—may share these characteristics under some conditions, but they are not built in, so they are rarely emphasized.

Recording media generally do not share these direct-contact characteristics; although specificity is possible, it is not built in. Materials may be designed and recorded for any degree of specificity, but they may also be designed more generally, and this is usually a necessity if the system is to achieve economies of scale.

Slide advance in radiovision is cued by slide number, or by short transition segments of music. Systems have also been used where pulses carried on a subcarrier of the main FM radio channel advanced slide projectors automatically. Under such a system, of course, all projection equipment at all receiving locations has to be identical. Since it is much more common that each location has its own type of projector, the manual methods are most often used.

### Audio Disc

When radio experienced its fastest growth as a mass medium, it was predicted that home phonographs and record players would be superseded. However, the convenience of having one's own library of recorded materials at home, with consequent freedom of access at any time, encouraged an even greater growth of the record industry. In 1967 the sales of phonographs were about twice those of radio receivers in dollar volume.[15] Nor has the sale of records been affected greatly by competition from audio tape. It is reported that records currently outsell prerecorded audio tapes four to one. To some extent this reflects the higher cost of tape over phonograph equipment; it may also reflect the greater convenience and accessibility of recordings when one need only set a needle to a specific cut on a disc, rather than run through a long tape to find the start of a desired number.

### Audio Tape

Recording of sound on magnetic tape was developed during

World War II in Germany; after the war, this technique came to form the basis of one of the most ubiquitous of American mass media. The first professional use of audio tape, significantly, was as a replacement for live radio production. The star of one of the most popular radio shows, Bing Crosby, found that adjusting his schedule to that of the radio audience was highly inconvenient. He contacted a small firm, Ampex, which was operating out of an old garage, experimenting with the new German method. Crosby found a method which turned out recordings that were all but indistinguishable from live radio. As a result, the Bing Crosby Show was the first to prerecord on tape, and the Ampex Corporation took a lead in the recording field which it has never entirely relinquished.

Given the necessary equipment, audio tape is the medium in which home recording is easiest for the average person. It is as much an individual recording medium as a mass playback medium. This is in contrast to audio disc, which was always a difficult medium in which to do home recording; even though equipment is available for this purpose, audio disc remains almost entirely a playback medium, with the recording done centrally for national distribution. Audio tape also has a very large sale as a playback medium, but practically all tape-playback equipment is also capable of recording. People with high-quality radio receivers find it convenient to record their own tapes from broadcasts.

The audio tape medium is based largely on the use of 1/4-inch tape, although other widths are also used for special multitrack purposes. There are several standard speeds, just as there are for audio disc; a higher speed improves quality while using more recording material. A slower speed saves tape but reduces quality. When the magnetic tape was first used in broadcasting, the tape ran at 30 inches per second for best quality, 15 inches per second for ordinary recording. In the 20 years since then, improvements in tape and recording heads first cut these speeds in half, then a few years later in half again. Seven and one-half inches per second is now the running speed that is generally used in broadcasting, and 3-3/4 is used for applications in which high quality is not so critical. A speed of 1-7/8 (half of 3-3/4) is also provided in the new portable recorders which use the reel-to-reel cassette. There is even a speed of 15/16 inches per second which allows a miniature recorder with 3-inch reels to record for four hours without changing reels. A new kind of tape, which is still in the laboratory stage, Crolyn tape (chromium dioxide is the magnetic medium) is expected to cut tape speeds in half once more.

## CLASS VII: PRINT MEDIA

Class VII media are capable of representing information only in alphanumeric characters and other symbols. Furthermore, they can present this program material in no other way than one character at a time. Thus they are time-based; the presentation of information, via those media, was for years limited to the rate at which such devices as mechanical teletype machines or electric typewriters could operate. Teletype printers operate at up to 100 words per minute, a slow reading speed, but sufficient if not too much is transmitted at a time. Teletype is thus frequently used in computer-controlled instructional systems, where the learner reads material as it is typed out and responds immediately by typing back answers.

The major uses of teletype in information transmission, however, involve the procedure of recording the information to be transmitted in advance on punched paper tape. It is then passed through a paper-tape reader, transmitted electronically, and recorded by a paper-tape punch at the receiving end. Paper tape can be read and punched at very much faster rates than typewriters can type; some of the tape-to-tape systems now on the market are capable of 750 words per minute, and some are capable of over 1000. This is about 16 times as fast as the average speaker talks. Once recorded on paper tape at the receiving end of the transmission system, the information may later be decoded by a paper-tape reader and typed off by an electric typewriter at 100 words per minute.

The advantage of all this is that the transmission system for the teletype requires a very narrow bandwidth—the same type of line, actually, that is used for ordinary telephone calls. Thus the costs of long-distance data transmission are the same as the costs of long-distance phone calls, and up to 16 times as much information can be transmitted.

# 6.
# Proposed Future Studies of Media

As presently planned, future writings from the Rand Corporation will discuss the uses to which instructional media are being put and the criteria which determine their appropriateness to the various uses. Such discussion will include accessibility to the user of various media and/or forms of media, the responsiveness of various media to changing needs and the adaptability of media to the individual needs of the learner.

Another equally important set of questions will concern the feasibility of different media under various conditions. This will involve discussions of cost and value, equipment standardization and reliability, demand for the medium and its acceptability to users.

As a practical help to media users in determining the relative feasibility of various alternative procedures in the production of program software, general cost models are being prepared for each media class. Future studies also involve media techniques, including techniques of integrating the use of a medium into a total learning environment, and techniques of expression in different classes of media. Techniques of melding sound and picture into a whole also will be explored. These matters will be discussed as much as possible in a universal way, drawing on as many media as appropriate for illustration and example. Considerable discussion will be devoted to the techniques of eliciting learner response via the media and means of providing feedback to that response so that more rapid and more lasting learning may become possible.

# Appendix

## LOCAL VERSUS CENTRAL PRODUCTION OF PROGRAM

## SOFTWARE IN INSTRUCTIONAL MEDIA SYSTEMS

The amenability of various media to local or home production of program software (films, tapes, etc.) has been discussed in Section 5, where the communication media are compared. Whether program materials should be exclusively professionally produced, or should also be created at the point of use by people who are essentially nonprofessional, is a standing issue among many media people, particularly in sound film, television, and to a lesser extent, filmstrip. Users of the printed page resolved this question decades ago with the acceptance of mimeograph, ditto, and later, the various photocopy devices. A large part of the printed materials used today consists of the relatively inexpensive, nonprofessionally produced forms. Although still regarded by book publishers as a threat, such materials appear to bear primarily a complementary rather than a replacement relationship to professionally produced books and pamphlets. These forms of the print medium have developed because the professional publishing industry could not satisfy the large variety of purely local, small-scale needs with anything near the inexpensiveness, the quick responsiveness to need and the specificity of local production.

In using the word "local" in regard to the production of program software for the communication media, more is expressed than pertinence to a limited place or area. Local production of media materials implies production by persons with other primary responsibilities, who are generally considered nonprofessionals in the production field. "Central" production, on the other hand, connotes production by a staff of professional craftsmen: experts in camera, lighting, laboratory techniques and all the other crafts that are required for professionalism in media program production. Generally, such production is centrally located in an educational system because it is expensive and must be spread over a wide base of use to find economic justification.

The terms "local" and "central" are relative. For example, a school district of a hundred schools may use some materials, such as textbooks, which are produced in New York and distributed nationally; it may use certain state-produced textbooks; it may install television studios to produce and distribute instructional television (ITV) lessons throughout the hundred schools; it may, as in Chicago, cluster six or twelve schools with similar peculiar needs and use television to share the resources of the cluster; it may localize to the level of the school, or, as in traditional self-contained classroom instruction, localize to the single teacher and classroom. There is production of media materials on all these levels, each being local in relation to the one above, each central to the one below.

Perhaps the most important point is that local production is not, generally, intended for reproduction and distribution, but will exist in only one copy if intended for group use and in only a few copies at most if intended for use in the individual mode.

This limited use of one of the most valuable characteristics of a communication medium, its broad reproducibility, means that there are no great economies of scale which, when costs of production can be divided over a large base of users, bring the cost per user down. The limited use base in local areas limits the funds that are available for program production and hence the possibility of maintaining professional personnel and facilities.

Local production is not necessarily limited to places which do not have professional production facilities. Again, the distinction is not alone in locale but in personnel who do the production. On the same airbase, for example, which houses a professional central production unit, there may also be local production going on. There may be a particular instructor or curriculum development group who have obtained access to a portable substandard-gauge video tape recorder and camera and are using television in their own small and limited way to improve their own teaching.

This trend toward production of program materials by the unprofessional is being felt today in all levels and types of education. High school and even elementary school children are making their own animated films.

Both film and TV came into communication use out of a background of several decades of existence almost exclusively as entertainment arts. This is not true of the minor media. This background strongly affects our approach toward program production in film and television and to a large extent in the still-picture and sound media as well, where the attempt is often made to emulate the artistic effectiveness of the major media.

When film, and later television, was expensive and steeped in the tradition of the entertainment arts, central production of high-quality program software seemed to be the only possible approach. Production techniques were inevitably compared with those of the familiar commercial products, and any local attempts at film or television production were almost invariably found wanting. We are now emerging from that period. Today the appearance of inexpensive video tape systems and the resurgence of 8mm film in the Super 8 form have begun to encourage production at the other end of the scale.

There is a continuum of costs, of complexity, and of certain kinds of effectiveness extending from the most elaborate to the very simplest production. It seems that the two ends of this continuum are receiving almost all the attention while the middle, where the great future probably lies, is being largely neglected.

The production of materials for instructional media is thus

usually undertaken under one of two conditions: great wealth or great poverty. The production of films, for example, when done centrally, with the whole nation (or the whole of a military service) as a base for distribution, can command traditional professional film budgets of $1000 to $1500 per program minute. At the other end of the scale, films are sometimes made by one instructor (or instructional team) for use in one course in one school on traditional amateur home-movie budgets where the cost of the film stock itself, a few dollars a minute, is considered the major item.

Since the present issue revolves about the usefulness of central versus local production, the two extreme ends of this scale, we will discuss some of the more obvious advantages and disadvantages of each. It is possible that intermediate methods could be found which could provide some of the advantages of both central and local production.

At the local level, there are needs which are specific to a given school or a given course (possibly even to a given instructor in some cases) and there are needs which are more general, common with other schools or other similar courses. The questions addressed here are, (1) Should local specific needs be met by local production or by central production? and (2) Should local common needs be met by local production or by central production? Under what conditions is local and under what conditions is central production best, and what criteria should be applied in making such judgments? These questions have been raised and are being debated in almost all areas where instructional media are used. Some of the advantages and disadvantages involved are enumerated below.

## ADVANTAGES OF LOCAL PRODUCTION
## OVER CENTRAL PRODUCTION

1. Local production can respond quickly to local need. This is important, since needs often appear suddenly. The small number

of man-hours that go into local production make this response possible; and long periods of waiting for official approval at various stages in the process are not necessary. The production cycle for instructional films in some of the military services, for example, runs regularly as long as two years between local request and completion of central production. Local production of portable video tape, on the other hand, can be completed in a matter of days, or weeks at the very most.

2. Local production can be highly specific; production can be tailored directly to instructional needs. This is due to the intimate knowledge of these needs by the film producers (since they themselves are the requesters and the future users of the materials). It is also due to the rather limited range of these needs. A film produced centrally for national distribution, by way of contrast, must try to satisfy a much wider range of needs in order to interest a larger market. Basic core materials for courses which are unique can best be produced locally.

3. Local production can be rapidly evaluated in practice and rapidly revised. A production may be put into immediate use; and, after observation of its instructional faults and shortcomings, revision can be made quickly. In the case of central production this procedure must often be done by several different groups of people at different places, accompanied by such hazards as the vagaries of verbal communication and the inevitable delays.

4. Local production is more democratic. The tradition which upholds the right of every small town to its own school system, curriculum and locally designed teaching materials is part of our democratic heritage. The same principle would be applied to the content of the instructional media if an even stronger principle, financial economy, did not conflict. Economic factors are primarily responsible for the national centralization of textbook publishing. So highly centralized has this instructional medium been that a few private publishers concentrated in an area of only a few square blocks in midtown Manhattan for many years designed and produced the printed learning materials for the majority of the nation's schools. The trend is now toward

decentralization. The development of centralized production in the other media may be resisted. Local production of instructional television lessons, for instance, with closed-circuit distribution within a local school district, appears to be the preferred school approach to the ITV medium, given favorable conditions of adequate funds and local acceptance.

5. Locally produced materials tend to be better used. An instructor who has had a hand in planning and producing or has actually appeared in a local media production not only begins its use with a clear idea of how he is going to integrate it with other instruction but generally believes solidly in its value. He has an interest in its success and unconsciously does all he can to maximize its effectiveness.

6. Locally produced materials can incorporate familiar surroundings and people. This can give the impression of greater relevancy, and is more likely to encourage students to identify with the persons and actions depicted.


## DISADVANTAGES OF LOCAL PRODUCTION

1. Local production is generally characterized by a low level of production quality. Since on-line instructional people are not generally skilled in the arts and crafts of media production, techniques are nonprofessional. Basic rules of film production, out of ignorance, are often breached. Lack of artistic skill or sensitivity may lead to pedantic, pedestrian results. On the other hand, this ignorance of traditional techniques can result in a naive freshness of approach that to the sophisticate, at least, may be appealing. To others it may just seem amateurish. However, it is a well-known principle of amateur production that the faults and shortcomings of a film are not obvious to its maker. In the case at hand, it must be remembered, the film maker is also the user: He is his own sponsor; he will be the one to evaluate the product. This local pride often seems to rub off on the local learners whose instructor or instructional team have produced the material. It has

been a frequent experience at institutions producing ITV lessons that tapes that have been considered highly effective in the local situation are declared unimpressive by instructors and learners elsewhere when they are offered for general distribution.

2. Local production is limited to simple studio techniques or to local locations and subjects. Central production, on the other hand, can cover subject matter which is too complex, too distant or too expensive to be available locally. Historical dramatizations in costume, or geographical presentations of life in other lands are poor subjects for local production.

3. The costs of long-range-effectiveness evaluation, such as measurement of job-performance proficiency, cannot be justified for limited local uses. Following up on graduates for months after graduation cannot be done by the local instructional team. As a result, only terminal performance at the end of a course is used to evaluate instruction and the effective use of the medium chosen.

4. Local production, specific to local need, generally has low commonality. This is the obverse of high specificity, discussed above as one of the advantages of local production. Low commonality/high specificity is also a disadvantage as well. If it is ever desired to make locally produced materials available to other instructional centers, it may be found that their specificity to local needs lowers their commonality and makes them less useful over a range of situations.

There is also a possibility that the last disadvantage, lack of generality, may not be as serious as it would seem. When local needs are met by local production, and *well* met because of a quick evaluation-feedback-revision cycle, these same needs will probably be well met wherever in instruction they may occur. Thus if another training center has some of the same needs in common, materials produced at the first center may satisfy very well that set of common needs and be useful and acceptable to the other center.

The local versus central production controversy is not an either/or question, however. It may be possible to do both local *and* central production, achieving the advantages of both. It is suggested that low-cost local production of instructional aids and instructional media be encouraged as much as possible. The resultant materials will thereby stand the maximum chance of being developed and validated quickly and have maximum value in meeting the specific *local instructional needs.* Materials so developed, if successful in local use, should then be examined for general applicability. If they are found to have usefulness elsewhere, the materials could be remade, following the validated and successful pattern, but utilizing professional techniques, quality graphics, etc., thus making them acceptable and useful to other schools.

*The issue of production values.* The argument that instructional materials benefit from professional techniques derives from the tendency of many people to evaluate the effectiveness of instructional communications in terms of criteria which have been derived from the entertainment field.

A general reason for this is that nearly all of us, in this culture, are long-time consumers of entertainment in the mass media, and have developed our own personal set of standards by which we judge whatever is displayed before us, either before we learn its specific purpose, or even after the purpose is known, since our private responses have a prior and subconscious strength. To be rated "good" it must have "pace," it must capture and hold our interest, it must look "professional," and the like.

A more specific reason affects the program producer's own evaluation of his work, and often undermines its effectiveness in achieving the results for which it is intended. This is the fact that most producers of instructional materials by virtue of previous occupation, or by virtue of the emphasis in their institution of training, evaluate any film they produce in terms of the criteria of the art-entertainment system. An instructional film which does not meet these criteria, however well it may satisfy its instructional purpose, is a source of no pride to its maker. When people are chosen to sit on boards of evaluation because they already know something about the medium involved, they frequently bring this approach with them.

The old-time movie producer who evaluated his films by showing them to his wife may have chosen, by luck, a fairly representative sample of his target audience, whose reactions may have been typical. Most of us evaluate films by our own reactions, even films for teaching in the primary grades. Probably only a fraction of people who evaluate instructional programs in the communication media are actually qualified to predict with any degree of certainty how successful a given program might be in achieving its instructional objectives. The idea of validating a program by actually testing it out in a sample learning situation and measuring its effect has only recently emerged, out of the set of valuable instructional innovations which came in the package called programmed instruction. The day may come when any instructional materials offered commercially will have to show such validation credentials before they are saleable.* At present, by and large, we do not look to the user system for the criteria with which we evaluate programs. We simply look at the program and evaluate it in a vacuum, so to speak, using whatever criteria we wish.

But there is another side to the question of the usefulness of artistic production techniques in instructional programs, which the following argument will unfold.

Bloom[16] lists three kinds of learning objectives—cognitive, psychomotor and affective. When the instructional media are used for cognitive objectives only, *which is most of the time,* it is necessary that the information which is to be conveyed be well organized, and the subject developed in small enough steps so as to be understandable to the intended learner but developed rapidly enough for each learner so it is not boring. Beyond this it is only necessary that what is to be seen is recognizable, what is to be heard is audible, what is to be read is legible and that there are not

---

*It has long been necessary for published standardized tests to give information about their validity and reliability if they are to be sold. (Validity: how closely the test measures what it purports to measure; Reliability: how consistently the test gives the same result when measuring the same thing.)

too many extraneous stimuli to distract the learner from attending to the message.

Objectives requiring the development of psychomotor skills outside the normal repertoire can only be fully attained through practice. It is mainly in the introductory aspects of skills instruction that media are useful, and that is because the objectives at that point are actually cognitive. One has to know what it is that he is learning to do, and why; he has to observe the kinds of responses he is intended to learn before he can begin to practice and learn them.

It is in helping to change people's attitudes that many consider the media to be most useful, and it is in the achievement of these objectives that artistic techniques can play their most important role. We are beginning to suspect that it is only to the extent that affective objectives are involved in cognitive instruction that production technique contributes to the effectiveness of knowledge lesson presentations.

Thus, those who argue that the broadcaster's art can make an important contribution to instructional television are really arguing (1) that there are some hidden affective objectives mixed up with the obvious cognitive ones, or (2) that even though there may be no stated affective objectives connected with the instruction, if artistic techniques are used, the learners will be in some way affected and that instruction will be enriched by the achievement of these unstated and unexpected affective behaviors.

The producer/artists, working in the broadcasting tradition, are experts in the art of moving people's emotions. They are skilled in techniques which create drama, involve the viewers and hold them in suspense until the situation is resolved. They know how to create visual pleasure through pattern design, arrangement of light and shadow and use of line; they are aware of the subtle connotations of style in lettering, graphic layout, set design and other visual elements. They believe the emotional attitude toward a subject that such artistry can evoke will remain with a person long after the details of the program have been forgotten.

Not all educational television or film producers, of course, are such artists. Many simply follow rules of technique that they have been taught, and succeed only in coating the program with a veneer of artistry without penetrating its content. It is not that the surface is unimportant, but simply that surface technique alone is meaningless. It is not how the performer looks, but what he does and says that is important. Nevertheless, how he looks doing or saying it can significantly enhance its effect.

Most producers feel they know more about how to achieve attitudinal changes in people than educators or instructors do, or at least they feel they are unique in being dedicated to that end. Thus, they view their role in the creation of instructional materials as an obligation to add affective objectives to the goals of the communication, even though such objectives have not been specified or planned prior to the production of the program. By so doing they believe they can create better instructional materials which will indirectly increase cognitive learning by increasing its motivation.*

There may be some truth in these opinions. Unfortunately, since the effects they claim lie in the realms of art, aesthetics and the affective domain, they are not always amenable to empirical study and validation. The researcher will say "Yes, very possibly, but can that be demonstrated?" Uncomfortably, attempts by researchers to find evidence to support the case for artistry have not been successful. Therefore, the instructional designer is in a position to choose either approach. If he dislikes or can't afford production values, he can point to the paucity of research findings which link artistic values to measured learning. If he is committed to the artistic approach, he can point to the same lack of evidence and to the frequently conflicting indications of the evidence available and conclude that his artistic intuition, having been successful in the past, will be his best guide in his present endeavor as well.

---

*Actually, what evidence there is points to an increased motivation, but a motivation to repeat the affective experiences, not a motivation toward cognitive learning.

## SUMMARY

Local versus central production is a big issue in the production of films and television programs; in all likelihood, it will make itself felt in the program production process of other instructional media as well. This issue is most likely to arise, however, in the media which are already mass media in their entertainment function: television, radio, audio disc and tape, and to some extent the printed page. It will be the least likely to arise in the purely information media, such as the microform film systems, and the individual transmission media: teletype and facsimile. Where there is the minimum possibility of designing and arranging space and time, or eliciting empathic responses with other humans, in media where no one has yet seen artistic techniques being used, no one will miss artistic qualities. In the other media, however, it is possible that local production, however effective it may be in achieving instructional objectives, will continue to be a lively issue.

# References

1. *Webster's Seventh New Collegiate Dictionary.* Springfield, Mass.: G. & C. Merriam Co., 1967.

2. McLuhan, Marshall. *Understanding Media: The Extensions of Man.* New York: McGraw-Hill, 1964, p. 174.

3. Chu, G. C. and Wilbur Schramm. *Learning From Television: What the Research Says.* Washington, D.C.: National Association of Educational Broadcasters, 1967.

4. *Ibid.*

5. McLuhan, *op. cit.,* p. 22.

6. Vetter, Richard H. *A Study of the Significance of Motion in Educational Film Communication,* Doctoral Dissertation, University of California at Los Angeles, June 1959.

7. Nuthman, C.F. *Time-Shared Interactive Computer-84 Controlled Educational Television (TICCET).* Bedford, Mass.: The MITRE Corporation, May 1968.

8. Vetter, *op. cit.*

9. Nuthman, *op. cit.*

10. Strandberg, Joel E., Evan R. Keislar and John D. McNeil. *A Talking Book System of Teaching Beginning Reading,* Final Report, Title VIIA, Project No. 1370, October 1967.

11. Seibert, Warren F. *A Preliminary Examination of the Educational Potential and the Future Assessment of Edufax.* University Park, Pa.: The Pennsylvania State University, June 1968.

12. *Audiovisual Equipment and Materials in U.S. Public School Districts.*
    Washington, D.C.: Bureau of Social Science Research, Inc., Spring
    1961, p. 75.

13. Jennings, Ralph M. The Potentials of Network Educational Radio.
    *NAEB Journal,* September/October 1966, pp. 45-56.

14. The Hidden Medium: A Status Report on Educational Radio in the
    United States. *NAEB Journal,* 1967.

15. *Statistical Abstract of the United States.* Washington, D.C.: U.S.
    Department of Commerce, 1968.

16. Bloom, Benjamin S., *et al. Taxonomy of Educational Objectives: The
    Classification of Educational Goals, Handbook 1: Cognitive Domain.*
    New York: David McKay, 1956.

# Index

# Selected Rand Books

Gurtov, Melvin. *Southeast Asia Tomorrow: Problems and Prospects for U.S. Policy.* Baltimore, Maryland: Johns Hopkins Press, 1970.

Kershaw, Joseph A., and Roland N. McKean. *Teacher Shortages and Salary Schedules.* New York: McGraw-Hill Book Company, 1962.

Leites, Nathan, and C. Wolf. *Rebellion and Authority.* Chicago, Illinois: Markham Publishing Company, 1970.

Meyer, John R., Martin Wohl, and John F. Kain. *The Urban Transportation Problem.* Cambridge, Massachusetts: Harvard University Press, 1965.

Nelson, Richard R., Merton J. Peck, and Edward D. Kalachek. *Technology, Economic Growth and Public Policy.* Washington, D.C.: The Brookings Institution, 1967.

Novick, David (Ed.). *Program Budgeting: Program Analysis and the Federal Budget.* Cambridge, Massachusetts: Harvard University Press, 1965.

Pascal, Anthony. *Thinking About Cities: New Perspectives on Urban Problems.* Belmont, California: Dickenson Publishing Company, 1970.

Sharpe, William F. *The Economics of Computers.* New York: Columbia University Press, 1969.

Sheppard, J.J. *Human Color Perception.* New York: American Elsevier Publishing Company, 1968.

The Rand Corporation. *A Million Random Digits With 100,000 Normal Deviates.* Glencoe, Illinois: The Free Press, 1955.

Williams, J.D. *The Compleat Strategyst: Being a Primer on the Theory of Games of Strategy.* New York: McGraw-Hill Book Company, 1954.